Politics and
Nuclear Power

Politics and Nuclear Power

ENERGY POLICY IN WESTERN EUROPE

Michael T. Hatch

THE UNIVERSITY PRESS OF KENTUCKY

For my parents

Copyright © 1986 by The University Press of Kentucky

Scholarly publisher for the Commonwealth,
serving Bellarmine College, Berea College, Centre
College of Kentucky, Eastern Kentucky University,
The Filson Club, Georgetown College, Kentucky
Historical Society, Kentucky State University,
Morehead State University, Murray State University,
Northern Kentucky University, Transylvania University,
University of Kentucky, University of Louisville,
and Western Kentucky University.

Editorial and Sales Offices: Lexington, Kentucky 40506-0024

Library of Congress Cataloging-in-Publication Data

Hatch, Michael T., 1945–
    Politics and nuclear power.

    Bibliography: p.
    Includes index.
    1. Nuclear industry—Government policy—Europe.
    2. Nuclear power plants—Government policy—Europe.
    3. Energy policy—Europe. I. Title.
    HD9698.E82H38   1986   333.79′24′094   85-29545
    ISBN 0-8131-1583-3

Contents

Acknowledgments

This study would not have been possible without the support and encouragement of numerous individuals to whom I owe much. Initial encouragement was provided through participation in the research project "Studies on International Scientific and Technological Regimes," directed by Ernst B. Haas and John Gerard Ruggie, housed in the Institute of International Studies at the University of California, Berkeley, and funded through the Rockefeller Foundation. A doctoral dissertation developed out of this project, financial support for the field work coming primarily from the German Fulbright Commission; additional support during the writing process was provided by the Institute of International Studies at Berkeley. The effectiveness of my research in Europe was greatly enhanced by the Deutsche Gesellschaft Fuer Auswaertige Politik, which opened its facilities to me throughout my stay in Bonn. Likewise, the assistance of the Atlantic Institute and its staff proved invaluable for my research in Paris. The resources subsequently required for rewriting and revisions were generously provided by the Politics Board at the University of California, Santa Cruz, and the Political Science Department of the University of California, Davis.

Many public officials in the Federal Republic of Germany, France, and the Netherlands gave freely of their time and opinions while being interviewed. To them, I am most grateful. My gratitude also goes out to John P. Holdren and Leslie Lipson who, as members of my dissertation committee, pa-

tiently read and commented on the earlier version of this manuscript. In the process of transforming this study from a dissertation into a book, the assistance received from reviewers and editors associated with the University Press of Kentucky has been invaluable.

In acknowledging debts, members of the Politics Board and the Comparative and International Studies O.R.A. at the University of California, Santa Cruz—where the bulk of the revisions were done—must receive special mention. As friends, they lightened an often arduous task and as colleagues, they provided critical comments. In particular, I would like to thank Michael Brown, who read and commented on the entire manuscript, and Isebill Gruhn, whose critiques of parts of the study were most useful. My greatest debt, however, is to Ernest B. Haas, who provided the intellectual guidance and unstinting support that made this study possible. What merit this study may have is due in large part to his influence; its shortcomings were beyond even his capabilities to remedy.

Finally, to my parents and friends go heartfelt thanks; their encouragement and support provided a constant source of renewal throughout the writing process.

Abbreviations

AEG	Allgemeine Elektrizitaets Gesellschaft
ARP	Anti-Revolutionaire Partij, Evangelische Volkspartij
BBC	Brown, Boverie & Cie
BBU	Bundesverband Buergerinitiativen Umweltschutz
BMFT	Bundesministerium fuer Forschung und Technologie
BMI	Bundesministerium des Innern
BMWi	Bundesministerium fuer Wirtschaft
CDA	Christen-Demokratisch Appel
CDF	Charbonnages de France
CDU	Christlich-Demokratische Union
CE	Coal Equivalent
CEA	Commissariat à l'Energie Atomique
CFDT	Confédération Française Démocratique du Travail
CFP	Compagnie Française des Pétroles
CGE	Compagnie Générale d'Electricité
CGT	Confédération Générale du Travail
CHU	Christlijk-Historische Unie
CNEN	Comitato Nazionale per l'Energia Nucleare
CNV	Christelijk Nationaal Vakverbond in Nederland
Cogema	Compagnie Générale des Matières Nucléaires
CPN	Communistische Partij van Nederland
CREST	Comité de la Recherche Scientifique et Technique
CSU	Christlich-Soziale Union
D'66	Democraten'66
DGB	Deutscher Gewerkschaftsbund
DWK	Deutsche Gesellschaft fuer Wiederaufarbeitung von Kernbrennstoffen
EC	European Community
ECSC	European Coal and Steel Community

ECU	European Currency Unit
EDF	Electricité de France
EEC	European Economic Community
ENA	Ecole Nationale d'Administration
ENI	Ente Nazionale Idrocarburi
EP	Ecole Polytechnique
ERAP	Entreprise de Recherche et d'Activité Pétrolière
Euratom	European Atomic Energy Community
Eurodif	European Gaseous Diffusion Enrichment Plant Study Group
FBR	Fast Breeder Reactor
FDP	Freie Demokratische Partei
FNV	Federatie Nederlandse Vakbeweging
GDF	Gaz de France
GDP	Gross Domestic Product
GNP	Gross National Product
GW	Gigawatt
HTR	High Temperature Reactor
IAEA	International Atomic Energy Agency
IEA	International Energy Agency
INB	Internationale-Natrium-Brutreaktor-Baugese-llschaft
INFCE	International Nuclear Fuel Cycle Evaluation
Interatom	Internationale Atomreaktorbau
KVP	Katholieke Volkspartij
kWh	kilowatt hour
KWU	Kraftwerk Union
LMFBR	Liquid Metal Fast Breeder Reactor
LNG	Liquid Natural Gas
LWR	Light Water Reactor
mbd	million barrels per day
mtce	million ton coal equivalent
mtpe	million ton petroleum equivalent
MW	Megawatt
NAM	Nederlandse Aardolie Matschappij
NKV	Nederlands Katholiek Vakverbond
NNPA	Nuclear Non-Proliferation Act
NPT	Non-Proliferation Treaty
NRW	North Rhine-Westphalia
NVV	Nederlands Verbond van Vakverenigingen
OAPEC	Organization of Arab Petroleum Exporting Countries

OECD	Organization for Economic Cooperation and Development
OPEC	Organization of Petroleum Exporting Countries
PCF	Parti Communiste Français
PEON	Commission Consultative pour la Production d'Electricité d'Origine Nucléaire
PPR	Politieke Partij Radikalen
PR	Parti Républicain
PS	Parti Socialiste
PvdA	Partij van de Arbeid
R&D	Research and Development
R,D&D	Research, Development and Demonstration
RPR	Rassemblement pour la République
RSK	Reaktorsicherheitskommission
RWE	Rheinisch-Westphaelische Elektrizitaetswerke
SEP	Samenwerkende Electriciteits-Productiebedriejven
SNR	Schneller Natriumgekuelter Reaktor
SPD	Sozialdemokratische Partei Deutschlands
SSK	Strahlenschutzkommission
TA-Luft	Technische Anleitung-Luft
TEG	Teilerrichtungsgenehmigung
tbd	thousand barrels per day
TMI	Three Mile Island
UAE	United Arab Emirates
UCN	Ultra-Centrifuge Nederland
URENCO	British-German-Dutch Enrichment Plant Ownership Company
VVD	Volkspartij voor Vrijheid en Democratie

1. Energy Policies and National Agendas

In recent years, the topic of energy has captured the attention—if not the imagination—of policymakers in the advanced industrialized countries of the West. The reason is obvious. Energy considerations have become central to the most pressing problems of modern society: economic growth, employment, and inflation. Economic growth in particular is intimately linked with energy consumption. Over the past thirty years, economic expansion in Western Europe, North America, and Japan has been fueled by an exponential increase in the consumption of oil. As long as oil supplies remained abundant and cheap, this development occasioned little concern. Once supply became problematical and prices skyrocketed, however, the implications for economic growth, employment, and inflation were forcefully brought home to policymakers and general public alike.

More recently, questions of environmental degradation have become prominent on political agendas. The most immediate worry has been the pollution of air and water, largely caused by current energy production and consumption practices. Yet, the already tangible impact on the Western quality of life pales beside predictions of environmental catastrophe if present practices are continued. Accordingly, on an ecologically finite earth, the consumption of fossil fuels must be drastically reduced and traditional patterns of economic growth eschewed.[1]

At one point, nuclear power was widely seen as the alternative to polluting, diminishing, and politically unreliable energy sources; but the promise of clean, abundant, and inexpensive nuclear energy now appears to have been ephemeral. Misgivings about the carcinogenic and genetic dangers attending the production of nuclear energy and the disposal of radioactive waste are increasingly being reflected in government policy. The result has been spiraling costs for the nuclear industry as it has faced more stringent safety standards, construction delays, and plant shutdowns.

Even if nuclear power were without environmental risk and considerably less costly than other fuels, however, its widespread use would still be problematic because of the danger of nuclear proliferation. Governments in the industrialized West are not eager to see fissionable materials in the hands of less stable regimes. Consequently, issues such as international safeguards and the transfer of peaceful nuclear technology have become subject to intense international negotiation.

Thus, energy can simultaneously affect decisions in disparate areas of policy such as military security, environmental protection, and economic welfare. Increasingly, energy appears to be defining many of the limits of political action in modern society.

In the following pages, I will examine the energy strategies of the Federal Republic of Germany, France, and the Netherlands. More specifically, I want to analyze the rise of energy policy to the top of national political agendas by the mid-1970s; and, within this context, the efforts of energy officials to formulate and implement ambitious nuclear power programs.

In general, the policies proposed by the energy officials of each country at the recognition of the energy crisis were remarkably similar. Traditional fuels such as coal and natural gas were to help hold down increases in oil consumption. Conservation, likewise, was to be stressed, although the commitment, at least initially, was largely rhetorical.

But nuclear power—the commercially available light water technology for the immediate future, the fast breeder reactor over the longer term—was to be the primary means of reducing dependence on imported oil. In the execution, however, national policy outcomes have been very different.

To understand why, we must go beyond the specific content of government energy policy to study the decision-making process itself. In the chapters that follow, close attention will be paid to policymaking. Several closely associated analytic concepts will be used to provide a common frame of reference for the comparison of the three countries' energy strategies. Let us take a brief look at these concepts before turning to a consideration of international energy policy.

COMPLEXITY, UNCERTAINTY, & CONSENSUAL POLITICS

In a groundbreaking work on comparative energy policy, Leon Lindberg describes the recent transformation in the type of actors and issues defining energy policy:

Most policymakers and analysts have traditionally defined energy policy as having to do with government and industry activities relative to the several stages (prospecting, mining, refining, transforming, transporting, marketing, and research and development) of the *supply* of the various forms of energy (coal, natural gas, petroleum, electricity) needed for individual and collective consumption and for industrial production. Increasingly, however, the boundaries of energy policy are expanding to include:
- The environmental and safety effects of producing and consuming energy;
- The capital requirements of various energy options and the complex interrelationships among economic growth, energy consumption and income and wealth distribution;

- The implications of various energy supply technologies for the structure of economic and political power within nations;
- The implications of existing and proposed patterns of energy production and consumption for national power and security, for international conflict, and for the future evolution of an increasingly interdependent global political and economic system.

[And within this expansion of energy policy boundaries are] new organizational actors (new governmental agencies and new elites) with somewhat different perceptions of the problem and responsibilities. More and more sectors of industry and more and more public agencies are involved and the problems of intergovernmental management . . . become more pressing. And since energy involves complex interdependencies, the policymakers of many other nations become de facto participants in any other nation's energy policy system . . . The environmental, employment, health, and safety consequences of one or another proposed energy technologies and foreign and security policy implications of import dependency have in the liberal democracies mobilized a variety of "outside" groups and previously inattentive publics . . . Ad hoc advocacy groups multiply, royal commissions and legislative commissions are established, antinuclear initiatives are placed on the ballot; court cases are filled.[2]

This seems to me a relatively accurate assessment of present energy policy. The implications for the political process are considerable.

In essence, what Lindberg here foreshadowed was the growing complexity of the energy policy. For our present purposes, *complexity* is defined as a function of the number of actors engaged in the political process, the number of objectives being pursued, and the degree to which these actors affect one another in pursuit of their objectives.[3] The coming pages will detail the specific responses of West Ger-

many, France, and the Netherlands to the growing complexity of the energy issue. We will see that the new approaches were much more comprehensive than the previous ones.[4] Somewhat paradoxically, however, a comprehensive response, in and of itself, may further exacerbate
the problem because of two closely associated factors: the
decline of the market as sovereign arbiter of energy policy decisions, accompanied by the expansion of governmental activity and responsibility throughout the energy
sector.

Indeed, where policymakers have opted for a comprehensive approach to energy policy, the primary reason for
change has been from the perceived dysfunctions of the
market: for example, overreliance on the international energy market for imported oil and the problems precipitated
by skyrocketing prices in the areas of inflation, employment,
economic growth, and balance of payments; the externalities
of energy use as they affect the environment; and the like.
Under circumstances where overt choices partially displace
the anonymous decisions of the marketplace, certain aspects
of the market that have made complex decisions more man-
ageable are lost.

Thus, a more comprehensive strategy affects the political system in a very fundamental way. Many areas previously regulated by the remote, self-adjusting mechanisms
of the market will now fall under government purview, increasing complexity by bringing new actors with their own
objectives into the expanded political arena. In other
words, the number of actors demanding participation will
increase appreciably with a comprehensive energy policy,
since many more groups and individuals will see themselves as affected.

If present-day energy policy must involve complex and
comprehensive approaches, it must at the same time be
conducted in an atmosphere of great uncertainty. In policy
spheres dominated by the complex interactions of many
actors pursuing often-competing objectives, cause and effect relationships have become increasingly difficult to de-

fine. The issues surrounding today's energy debate have
generated little agreement:

*   What are the problems to be addressed—impending eco-
    logical disaster, declining supplies of conventional fuels,
    the increased cost of fuels, growing dependence on foreign
    energy supplies?
*   What are the causes—profligate practices of advanced
    industrial countries, the finiteness of conventional energy
    resources, the machinations of OPEC, the manipulations
    of the oil industry, the ineptness of government interven-
    tion, perhaps government intervention itself?
*   Where are the solutions to be found—in a fundamental
    transformation of modern lifestyles, increased efforts to
    conserve energy, development of alternative energy
    sources, freeing the forces of private enterprise?
*   What are the socio-political implications for a society that
    foregoes traditional economic growth; the exact relation-
    ships between energy consumption and economic growth,
    the precise trade-offs between proposed alternative en-
    ergy technologies' cost, environmental impact, political
    and social structures, and so forth?

While many groups active in the energy debate may
believe that they have identified the causal links in the
energy concatenation, agreement among them is spotty at
best. The broad differences over the nature of the energy
problem and the choices required to rectify it have proved
unamenable to compromise, thus frustrating the movement
toward consensus that is preferred in democratic polities. In
the coming pages, we will analyze the effect of these uncertainties on the ability of government to build the consensus
needed for political action.

OVERVIEW OF THE BOOK

The guiding question of this study is: what pushed nuclear power to the top of the political agenda in the Federal
Republic of Germany, France, and the Netherlands, yet led
to very different outcomes? To address this question, we

must first look beyond a strict analysis of the nuclear issue to examine the context of overall energy policy and its evolution over time. Further, to assess the forces shaping the three countries' energy strategies, we must briefly review developments in the international energy market in the years since the Second World War. This is the task of the following two chapters.

Chapter 2 looks at the changes in the structure of the world market, the effects of those changes on the price and supply of oil, and the responses to such changes at the national level through the early 1970s. These responses were characterized by a general preference for allowing the international market to determine the general shape, direction, and content of energy policy. Chapter 3 focuses on the national energy strategies formulated in response to the OPEC revolution. In contrast to the earlier period, energy policy is defined much more comprehensively and government is given an active, central role in its execution. This period also saw nuclear power given a central role to play in reducing dependence on imported oil. Finally, we will see how the transformation of energy strategies in the mid-1970s resulted in certain changes in overall decision making that led to the different outcomes examined in this book.

Chapters 4 and 5 offer the heart of the analysis, exploring the various dimensions of nuclear policy in West Germany. Chapter 4 examines the unraveling of political consensus on nuclear power as various actors were introduced into the policymaking process. Chapter 5 analyzes subsequent government efforts to resolve the developing political stalemate over nuclear power, as policy became mired in domestic electoral politics and the entanglements of an international debate over nuclear proliferation. The situation in Germany was strongly affected by the structure of the political system and its impact on nuclear policy.

Chapters 6 and 7 compare German nuclear policy with that of two other European countries. Chapter 6 examines nuclear policy in France. Although France shared certain characteristics with West Germany—a strong commitment to nuclear power and comparable levels of domestic opposition throughout much of the 1970s—the French state was not deflected from its policy of rapid nuclear expansion. More similar to the German outcome was the Dutch case. Chapter 7 details how implementation of a proposed Dutch nuclear program has been stalled for a decade as government officials have sought the type of broad political consensus valued in their polity. Again, the political system of each country played a crucial role in structuring its nuclear debate.

Chapter 8 briefly analyzes the factors responsible for the rise of the nuclear power issue to the top of the political agenda and the differing abilities of governments to implement their nuclear programs. We see that the transition from the more limited, ad hoc approach to energy policy, which relied primarily on the market, to a comprehensive, long-term energy strategy, in which government played a more central role, had the effect of transforming the nuclear controversy from a scattered, local phenomenon to a national debate that engaged the major political, social, and economic institutions of each country. The reasons for this, I will argue, had much to do with the corresponding change from an incremental to a more synoptic approach to policymaking, an approach that elevated the policymaking structure itself to a position of crucial importance.

2. World Energy Markets and National Policy

In order to assess properly the forces now shaping the energy debate that began in the 1970s, we must look at the antecedents within the context of developments in the international energy market. In this chapter, I will first examine the structure of the world energy market as it has evolved since the end of the Second World War, focusing specifically on changes in the oil company/producer country relationship and their effect on the price and supply of oil. Second, I will consider the response of national energy officials to these changes through the early 1970s, taking special note of how far policymakers relied on market mechanisms in the conduct of energy policy or opted for governmental intervention.

FROM CARTEL TO OLIGOPOLY: 1945–70

Throughout much of the twentieth century, the world energy market has been shaped largely by the policies of the international oil majors—Exxon, Mobil, Socal, Texaco, Gulf, Royal Dutch Shell, British Petroleum (BP), and Compagnie Française de Pétrole (CFP). As early as the 1920s, efforts to structure this market along the lines of a cartel were undertaken, as the international majors negotiated explicit arrangements to regulate the production and marketing of oil worldwide. Central to these cartel arrangements were the so-called "Red Line Agreement," which established means of controlling levels of production within the Middle East as well as access to that production, and the "Achnacarry Agreement" or "As Is Agreement of 1928," which defined the market shares to be allocated to participating members.[1] Once fully operative, these cartel arrangements served to stabilize a market earlier characterized by frequent periods of overproduction and collapsing oil prices.

Following the Second World War—as national governments in Western Europe, the United States, and Japan became increasingly interested in the operations of the international oil market—the cartel framework gave way to an oligopolistic organization. That is, explicit collusion at the expense of competition was no longer practised, but considerable competitive self-restraint in commercial activities was displayed by the international majors.[2]

Through the 1950s, vigorous competition in the world oil market was moderated by the international majors' exclusive control of oil production in the Middle East. Because of concessions granted by local governments to the oil companies—often stipulating exclusive production rights for periods of up to sixty years or more—the majors could exclude potential competitors from the most profitable area of oil production. Thus able to regulate production and control access to crude oil, the international majors informally restricted price competition, thereby keeping prices at an artificially high level. By the late 1950s, however, certain developments had begun to undermine the majors' control of production and distribution.

One minor factor was the entrance of the Soviet Union into the world petroleum market. Soviet oil furnished independents and state oil companies with a limited supply of crude oil, but this alone was not enough to pose a long-term threat to the majors. More important was the acquisition of concessions in the Middle East by independent and state-owned oil companies, which provided the breakthrough needed to challenge the position of the majors. By agreeing to more advantageous deals for the producer countries, these companies gained a crude oil base that enabled them to compete more effectively with the international majors for customers on the world market. For example, rather than the fifty/fifty concessions traditionally given by the majors, joint venture agreements offered a seventy-five/twenty-five split of production revenue shares. Finally, the imposition of import quotas on oil in the United States after 1957 left Western Europe virtually the only other major oil market capable of absorbing the new oil production flooding the market.

The consequences of these events were swift in coming: increased competition, with a subsequent breakdown in the informal pricing arrangement among the majors. The extent to which the oligopolistic structure of the world market changed over the course of the 1960s is illustrated in the following figures: in 1957, the eight international majors controlled 91.7 percent of OPEC production; by 1970, approximately two hundred companies had entered the international market, with their output representing about 20 percent of OPEC production.[3] As the international majors fought to protect their traditional markets from the aggressive pricing policies of their new competitors and, at the same time, compete with the independents and one another for growing markets in Western Europe, the price of oil fell dramatically: in 1959 the posted price dropped from $2.08 per barrel to $1.80, while the actual selling price declined even farther (1959, $1.50; 1965–67, $1.00–1.25; and 1969, $1.00–1.10).

The precipitous fall in oil prices, combined with the prospect of further increases in supply and the attractive physical properties of oil—its ease of transport and use, compared to coal—held important implications for those European countries that had relied on coal to fuel their reconstruction after the war.

ENERGY POLICY IN WEST GERMANY

Energy policy in the Federal Republic of Germany throughout most of the postwar era has been a series of responses to developments in the nation's coal industry, an important and prominent element in the domestic economy. The largest indigenous energy source in Western Europe, domestically produced coal dominated German energy patterns (see Tables 1 and 2 in Appendix). More than 500,000 people were employed in the coal industry throughout the 1950s, with millions more indirectly affected by coal. Most of the industrial activity associated with coal and steel production was concentrated in one area, the Ruhr basin.

With a burgeoning demand for coal to fuel economic recovery, the coal industry appeared to be entering an era of prosperity in the 1950s: between 1950 and 1957, coal production had increased 20 percent and employment had jumped from 536,800 to 604,000 (see Table 3 in Appendix). Over the next decade, however, the coal industry went through a crisis from which it never completely recovered.

With the aforementioned changes in the world energy market by the 1950s, German coal became increasingly uncompetitive with oil. Whereas the price for German coal had remained relatively stable for the ten years between 1957 (DM 63.29 per ton) and 1966 (DM 67 per ton), the price for fuel oil went from DM 95.20 per 1,000 CE (coal equivalents) in 1957 to DM 37.36 in 1966 (see Table 4 in Appendix). The effects were devastating. Between 1957 and 1968, employment fell from 604,000 to 272,000 as conversion from coal to oil accelerated. Hard coal dropped to only 34 percent of total energy consumption in 1968 as opposed to almost 70 percent in 1957. Stockpiles of unsold coal fluctuated wildly over the same period (1957, 1 million tons; 1959, over 17 m; 1963, under 4 m; 1966, over 20 m).[4] No German government could ignore the political implications in these figures.

Beginning in 1959, the federal government, under increasing pressure from the so-called Ruhr lobby, undertook a series of measures designed to counteract, or at least slow, the transition from coal to oil. The Ruhr lobby is a unique constellation of forces that gives the coal sector substantial political clout. Industrially, coal companies in Germany have traditionally been closely associated with powerful steel interests (steel holdings produced over 52 percent of German coal). Coal miners are represented by one of the larger and more influential labor unions in the Federal Republic (*I. G. Bergbau und Energie*), which, in addition, maintains very close ties with a major political party, the Social Democrats (SPD). North Rhine-Westphalia, one of the economically and politically most powerful of the eleven Laender in the Federal Republic, is where these industrial activities are concentrated. The North Rhine-Westphalia government, therefore, has treated very seriously the problems of the coal sector.

The first major government effort was an informal government attempt to establish a coal-oil cartel in which the international majors committed themselves not to sell heavy fuel oil (the most direct competitor to coal) under the price level as determined on the world market and recognized by the cartel. This approach was quickly abandoned, however, as outsiders not belonging to the cartel began to take over an appreciable portion of the German fuel oil market by underbidding the cartel price.

Following the collapse of the cartel, the government tried more direct action. A 1960 law levied a tax on fuel oil, but this too failed as the price increase evidently had not been passed on to the consumers by the companies.

A third tack was pursued in the mid-1960s. The government attempted to promote the use of coal in the specific sectors of power generation and steel: power generation laws (*Verstromungsgesetze*) were passed that offered various incentives to construct or extend the use of power plants committed to the burning of coal. At the same time, coking coal subsidies were provided to the steel industry. Although somewhat more effective than their predecessors, these measures were not enough to offset the cumulative monetary and social costs of declining coal sales and rising unemployment.[5]

One further salvage attempt was made by the federal government in the late 1960s. Legislation was offered to initiate a wholesale restructuring of the coal industry.

Drawing on the lessons of the unsuccessful 1963 efforts to rationalize the coal industry, a single private corporation unifying all of Ruhr coal was created in November 1968—Ruhrkohle A. G. In contrast to earlier government policy intended to maintain coal production at a specific level, the task of Ruhrkohle was to make German coal as competitive as possible, which meant drastic reductions in production capacity and output, or, more bluntly, the closure of the less efficient mines.[6]

Thus, German energy policy was, essentially, coal policy. Energy officials took action in the oil sector only as heavy fuel oil came to compete directly with coal for customers. Government policy was not to concern itself at all with overall consumption patterns or with their future developments. The government preferred the market to be the final arbiter in such matters. Even the complete restructuring of the coal sector, as represented in Ruhrkohle, signified acceptance of market forces and a hope to restore coal eventually to the marketplace.

FRANCE AND ENERGY PLANNING

The conclusion of the Second World War left France a country psychologically humiliated by its rapid collapse before the German invasion and morally compromised by the Vichy collaboration. It is not surprising, therefore, that the new French leadership put the highest priority on the restoration of France's former "grandeur." According to Charles de Gaulle, this required that France become a "great industrial power."[7] What has been described as "stagnant, non-competitive industries associated with the sclerosis and decadence of the interwar period" was to be transformed.[8] Within this context, a small body of planners headed by Jean Monnet formulated a plan to modernize French industry. The Plan Monnet, in turn, was to articulate the content and direction of French energy policy.

Central to the plan's strategy was intensive development of coal and hydroelectric power—a choice representing a conscious preference for national energy sources in the immediate post-war period. Among the reasons were the large amounts of energy required for reconstruction and the scarcity of energy throughout Europe at the time. In addition, this preference reflected the high political value attached to the restoration of French autonomy by Gaullists and others.

At the same time, the most relevant energy sectors were nationalized. Under the nationalization laws of 1946, virtually the entire coal sector came under the public ownership of Charbonnages de France (CDF). Electricité de France (EDF) was given monopoly rights in the production, transport, and distribution of electrical energy. In addition, Gaz de France (GDF) was set up to control all activities in the gas sector.

By 1952–53, reconstruction of the basic sectors outlined in the Plan Monnet had pretty much been completed. In 1954–57, the Second Plan therefore placed greater emphasis on the construction of thermal power plants because of the high costs associated with hydroelectric production. Sixty-five percent of all increased production capacity was to be covered by thermal plants, 35 percent by hydroelectric. However, most French mines reached their maximum capacity toward the end of the Second Plan, with coal production in France peaking at 60 mt in 1958. As energy consumption outstripped domestic coal production, there was a rapid increase in the importation of coal and oil (see Table 5 in Appendix).

In the early 1950s, as the importance of oil in French energy supply was becoming more apparent, efforts were under way to help assure control of the domestic petroleum sector. In 1951 a system requiring special authorization for importing and refining oil was reimposed.[9] Further, the Bureau de Recherches de Pétrole was created by the state to finance exploration in France's overseas territories. Finally, in an attempt to control the distribution of oil products more effectively, a CFP subsidiary—Total—was established in 1955.[10]

Together, these measures served the purpose of the Sec-

ond Plan and its stress on developing the petroleum as well
as coal and electrical sectors by expanding the domestic
refining industry and intensifying exploration within
France and the franc zone—primarily North Africa and
Gabon. The intention was not only to help assure energy
supply but also to improve France's balance-of-payments
position. Somewhat unrealistically, the Second Plan projected a 40 percent increase in the volume of exports with no
increase in the volume of imports, a feat to be made possible
through anticipated developments in such import-substi-
tution industries as oil production.[11]

The Second Plan, again, largely defined the content and
direction of French energy policy through the mid-1950s. As
in the Plan Monnet, public investments were focused on
developing national energy sources, although at times with
certain shifts in emphasis. Maximizing coal production and
expanding electrical power generation (but with thermal
rather than hydroelectric plants) remained priorities; exploring for oil and gas within France and the franc zone
gained in prominence; and accelerating development of a
domestic refining capacity received greater attention.

French energy policy as articulated in the Third Plan
(1958–61) maintained the orientation toward developing
national energy resources. Circumstances, however, caused
the major guidelines of the plan to be virtually ignored by
the public officials responsible for energy policy.

In 1958 and 1959, energy demand in France was stagnating because of a slump in the economy.[12] In addition,
changing conditions in the international oil sector, combined with continued worldwide increases in coalmining
productivity, was leading to an energy glut rather than
gap. As a consequence, French coal declined steadily in
competitiveness against imported oil. Between 1958 and
1965, the price of coal for industrial use increased 19 percent while the price of heavy fuel oil for industrial use
declined 17 percent; the price of coal for domestic use increased 33.8 percent while the price of heating oil for
domestic use declined 12.7 percent.[13] The resulting drop in

oil prices, accompanied by a decline in the price of American coal, presented French officials with an uncomfortable dilemma. Should they continue to emphasize the development of secure national energy supplies, despite their cost and scarcity, or should they place greater reliance on abundant, inexpensive, imported energy at a time when the international competitiveness of French industry was being seen as increasingly critical?

This concern with the economic and political wellbeing of France was due in large part to French membership in the European Community. As a consequence of the systematic dismantling of tariff barriers among the member states of the European Community and the negotiation of common external tariffs beginning in 1959, the French economy for the first time in decades was exposed to international competition.

A decision came swiftly in the form of the Plan Jeanneney, a program adopted in June 1960 to reduce French coal production substantially. Discarding the optimistic goal of 63 mt set less than two years earlier, the new plan called for closing unprofitable and inefficient mines in areas such as the Centre and Midi to cut production to 53.5 mt in 1961.

Thus, the Third Plan and its energy policy was brushed aside. Rather than relying primarily on domestic coal, increased hydroelectric production, and development of indigenous oil and natural gas sources, the government would pursue improved international competitiveness by increased consumption of inexpensive, imported oil.[14] Market considerations would serve as the overriding, if not the sole, criteria in energy policy decisions throughout the 1960s.

With oil prices declining steadily on the world market during the 1960s and coal production dropping at an accelerated pace, the French oil sector expanded rapidly.[15] The objective of energy policy came to be the promoting of the international competitiveness of French industry. However, this market logic did not mean less state intervention in the petroleum sector, nor did it mean complete abandonment of efforts to retain some degree of energy independence, although the concept as defined by French officials assumed somewhat different connotations in the 1960s than it had carried in the 1950s—or would acquire in the 1970s.

Reflecting more general concerns pervasive in France at the time (le "défi Américain"), energy independence came to be defined not only by the ratio between domestic production and energy imports but also increasingly by the threat of international ("Anglo-American") oil companies dominating the domestic petroleum market. The response of French officials was twofold: first, they established new import, refining, and distribution quotas to allocate a larger share of France's rapidly expanding market to French companies and to reserve a larger share of France's rapidly expanding oil sector; second, they moved to acquire crude oil production for French companies independent from that of the international majors. The new distribution quotas established in 1965 allotted 52.9 percent of the domestic market in 1965 and 54.4 percent in 1968; the refining quota, covering a ten-year span beginning in 1965, was set at 61.3 percent. In addition, the state required that at least 90 percent of all petroleum products distributed domestically be refined in France.

With loss of ownership in the Saharan oil fields after Algerian independence (1962), the French government pursued a strategy of state-to-state negotiations with producer countries. In December 1965, ERAP—a totally state-owned oil company—was created from existing smaller state oil entities for implementation of this strategy. An initial agreement was concluded with the Algerian government that same year, establishing a so-called position privilégiée for French oil interests in Algeria (although the prices set for Algerian oil were somewhat higher than those prevailing on the world market).[16] Subsequent agreements were concluded between ERAP and Iran, Iraq, Saudi Arabia, and Libya, but these were less important, as 80 percent of ERAP's crude oil production came from Algeria.

Thus, although the objectives of French energy policy in the oil sector throughout the 1960s were still being stated in terms of "security of supply" or "energy independence," they actually had less to do with the total amount of domestic energy consumption that was supplied by imports than by control over the domestic oil market and assured "French" crude oil production. And although this required pervasive state intervention, the state placed few constraints on the function of the international market. As Saumon and Puiseux point out, these various methods of state intervention "were never used to limit or direct the use of petroleum products" (p. 141). Indeed, although both major French oil companies—CFP and ERAP—were nominally controlled by the state, they followed essentially the same policies as the international majors: maximize sales, stimulate demand through pricing policies, and the like.

In short, as France's economy began to open up with the creation of the Common Market, state actions in the energy sector seemed less and less guided by a plan. With oil prices dropping on the world market and the international competitiveness of French industry supplanting energy independence as the major concern of public officials, market forces increasingly dictated the patterns of French energy consumption throughout the 1960s.

Official expression of this change in priorities was reflected in the 1968 report of PEON, Annex 7: "It is futile to hope to attain . . . total independence at a time when the national economies are dependent upon each other in an ever-increasing manner. Then what is independence? It is possible to define the potential for economic independence as the capacity to maintain economic competitiveness for the long term and on an international scale, without letting this capacity be at the mercy of decisionmaking centers that would no longer be controlled by a national or multinational collectivity."[17] In other words, the principal criterion of independence is economic competitiveness.

ENERGY AND THE ECONOMY IN THE NETHERLANDS

In the years immediately following the Second World War, Dutch policymakers were confronted with a cluster of economic problems that required prompt attention:

- Approximately one-third of the Netherland's national wealth had been lost under German occupation.
- Important traditional trade patterns had been seriously disrupted by the war; Indonesia, Holland's principal dependency before the war, became independent, and Germany, one of the country's largest pre-war markets, faced major rebuilding.
- The population of the Netherlands was growing at an uncomfortably rapid rate—the working population of the Netherlands increased approximately 12 percent between 1950 and 1960.
- Its industrial base was not as highly developed as was its European neighbors'.

The options available to government officials were severely circumscribed. Although modernization of the traditionally important agricultural sector was required, mechanization only exacerbated the acute employment situation, and the surplus labor could not be absorbed by increases in industrial production because the domestic economy provided too small a market. Taking into account such constraints, Dutch officials finally adopted a strategy of industrial development that emphasized exports. To guarantee the competitiveness of Dutch products on the world market, the government pursued an active incomes policy to hold down wages and prices.

The success of this strategy was reflected in the performance of the Dutch economy over the next two decades: between 1949 and 1960, the volume of industrial exports rose approximately 400 percent; overall, net national income had risen from Fl 17.06 billion in 1950 to Fl 61.69 billion by 1965; and the gross domestic product increased at a rate of 4.8 percent a year between 1950 and 1960 and 5 percent a year from 1960 to 1965.[18] Along with this success went the search for energy sources to fuel the economic expansion.

As in both France and the Federal Republic of Germany, in the Netherlands reconstruction of the economy following the Second World War was based primarily on restoration of domestic coal production, though the ratio of production to total consumption represented a somewhat higher level of energy dependence than that of either France or West Germany.[19] By the late 1950s, however, the Dutch coal industry, like that in other European countries, was encountering the problems caused by the dramatic decline in oil prices and American coal prices.

In contrast to West Germany, where the government—at least initially—had neither the means nor the inclination to intervene directly in the marketplace, Dutch officials possessed several of the technical resources required to protect their coal sector from competing coal imports, had the government desired to do so. In 1902, the Dutch government had established the State Mines (*Staatsmijnen*) to prevent foreign control of the coal industry. Through the mid-1960s, State Mines controlled 60 percent of production; the remainder was owned primarily by steel companies (approximately 25 percent). Management of the government's wage and price policy had given officials the experience necessary to administer effectively a program designed to save the coal industry. Yet, aside from a few rather insignificant measures, such as discontinuing the issue of licenses for coal imports from the United States and promulgating requirements for minimum stocks by oil marketers, the government did virtually nothing to shield domestic coal from foreign competition or even to slow the switch to imported oil. Instead, with the rapid displacement of coal by oil, successive measures were formulated to eliminate domestic coal production. In 1966 an agreement was concluded between the Dutch government and State Mines on output reduction, measures followed in 1969 by a government announcement that all state mine production would end in 1973 and that all private mines would close by 1975. These figures tell the story: coal production fell from 11.4 mt to 6.7 mt between 1957 and 1968; employment in the industry declined at an even faster rate: from 47,245 in 1957 to 18,700 in 1968.

In deciding to expose the country's chronically uncompetitive coal sector to the full force of international competition, the government accepted an immediate increase in Dutch energy dependence and substantial economic dislocations in the coal mining province of Limburg. The reasons for strategy that permitted the elimination of an entire industrial sector can be found in the role alternative energy sources had begun to play in Dutch economic policy.

Holland's economic prosperity has long been linked to foreign trade. Possessing few natural resources, the Netherlands has imported almost all of its raw materials and paid for them largely through the sale of finished products abroad. By the early 1960s, the value of imports had come to represent approximately 50 percent of the national income, with exports slightly less.[20] In this light, growing energy dependence as a consequence of increasing energy imports appeared insignificant, especially as the Netherlands was in an excellent position to benefit from transformations in the international energy market then underway.

First, Royal Dutch Shell, one of the largest and most powerful oil companies in the world, had its headquarters in the Netherlands and Dutch interests held 60 percent of the shares. With Dutch Shell occupying an extremely important position in the Dutch economy, both tended to profit from increasing oil trade.

Second, the port of Rotterdam was ideally situated to serve the rapidly expanding oil markets of central and northern Europe. The international majors were reassured by the Dutch government's refusal to prop up its ailing coal sector, which signaled its commitment to a freely competitive energy market, and by the importance of Royal Dutch Shell in the country. Thus, corporate investment soon pushed Rotterdam to the forefront of the international oil trade. Extensive transshipment, storage, and petrochemical facilities were developed, along with what was to become the largest refining complex on earth. Because approximately 80 percent of the volume passing through Rotterdam was destined for re-export—much of it in the form of refined products—the income and jobs these activities added to the Dutch economy were significant.

Third, as we saw earlier, competitiveness on the international market was perceived as the key to economic prosperity. Industrial production for the world export market was to provide the domestic employment to accommodate an increasing work force. And while the government's incomes policy was the major tool used to hold down production costs, a policy allowing low-cost energy imports to displace more expensive domestic coal fitted well with such an export strategy.[21]

Fourth, in an energy development of equal or greater importance, a huge natural gas field was discovered in the province of Groningen. In 1959, the exploration efforts of a company formed jointly by Shell and Esso—NAM or *Nederlandse Aardolie Matschappij*—had finally paid off with the natural gas finds of the Slochteren field and the acquisition of the concession to all of Groningen by 1963, although at a cost. Under Dutch mining law, no concession had to be granted until oil or gas had been found; the government, therefore, was able to dictate the terms of the concession. In this case, the oil companies were forced to take on the state as a partner. Dutch State Mines took 40 percent interest in NAM, which was to be responsible for exploration, production, and marketing of the Slochteren gas and each of the international majors received 30 percent. Gasunie, which was to handle inland transportation and wholesale distribution of the gas from all sources, was jointly controlled by Shell (25 percent), Esso (25 percent), Dutch State Mines (40 percent), and the Dutch government (10 percent).[22]

Initially NAM formulated a sales strategy for an orderly marketing of the natural gas, which was to discipline the rate of expansion.[23] But with the price of oil cheap and continuing to decline, the recent commercial discoveries of natural gas in the North Sea, and developments in the

United States during the early 1960s that fostered expectations of abundant, safe nuclear energy within twenty years,
this strategy was quickly supplanted by plans to exploit the
gas as quickly as possible. Massive long-term export contracts were concluded with French, Belgian, German, and
Italian companies, so that, by 1973, natural gas exports
accounted for 48 percent of total domestic production. With
the lowering of internal prices, the domestic conversion to
natural gas, particularly in most end uses, was very swift.
Where in 1965 oil had 65 percent of domestic energy consumption and natural gas had 5 percent, by 1973, natural
gas and oil had equal shares of 47 percent.

Thus market forces largely dictated energy policy choices
in the Netherlands between 1950 and the early 1970s. The
results can be seen in the accompanying table.[24]

The state coal industry was sacrificed to cheaper energy
sources on the world market and to increasing interests in
the gas sector. Official energy policy objectives remained
unarticulated, although energy costs and their effects on
economic activity were accorded primary importance. Because the international energy market appeared to be functioning satisfactorily for Dutch interests, the government
made few systematic efforts to anticipate future developments.

THE TRANSFORMATION OF THE
WORLD ENERGY MARKET, 1970–73

Between 1970 and 1973, the international energy market
underwent a rapid, thorough transformation. The declining
prices that had characterized the buyers' market of the
1960s were being replaced by a sellers' market in which the
price of oil rose to levels that were considered at the time
exorbitant. Further, the relationship between oil company
and producer country was being altered fundamentally.
Both changes were closely tied to the growing influence of
OPEC.

In virtually all advanced industrial countries of the West

Dutch Energy Consumption Patterns in Percentages of
the Total

	Coal	Oil	Natural Gas
1950	76.6	22.8	0.7
1955	66.9	32.3	0.8
1960	49.2	49.3	1.5
1965	30.0	64.9	5.1
1970	10.5	57.1	32.4
1971	7.6	52.4	40.0
1972	5.8	49.1	45.0

and Japan, consumption of oil had been increasing almost
exponentially. The United States was no exception, but
there was one major difference. One of the largest markets
in the world, the United States had been largely self-sufficient, where Western Europe and Japan relied heavily on
imports of oil from the Middle East. The relatively small
amounts of oil imported by the United States—less than 10
percent of total energy consumption in 1970—came primarily from nearby Canada and Venezuela. This situation began to change by the early 1970s.

Because of price controls and the depletion of domestic
fields, oil production in the United States was starting to
level off. In addition, Venezuela had begun to limit production in order to conserve reserves, and Canada had started to
impose ceilings on exports. Unable to meet its burgeoning
demand for oil from these former sources, the United States
increasingly went outside the Western Hemisphere. By
1973, 35 percent of oil and natural gas (15 percent of its total
energy consumption) was imported, with most of it coming
from the Middle East.[25] Given the already large and growing requirements in Western Europe and Japan for Middle
Eastern oil, the stage was set for oil producers to exploit the
situation.

The Organization of Petroleum Exporting Countries
(OPEC) was created in 1960 in response to the drop in oil
prices. Although somewhat successful in stabilizing reve-

nues, the member countries were unable to bring about any price increase, largely because of surplus supplies persisting through much of the 1960s.[26] However, in the wake of a military coup in Libya in September 1969 that placed Muammar Qaddafi in charge of the country, this began to change.

Basing its claims on Libya's proximity to the major markets of Western Europe and the desirability of Libyan low-sulfur crude in those markets because of the importance of the environment as a political issue in the West, the Qaddafi government demanded a price increase for its oil. Exploiting the vulnerability of several independents in Libya—Occidental in particular—to threats of reduced oil production, loss of concessions, and the like, the Qaddafi government finally obtained more favorable terms from Occidental in September 1970. The other independents as well as the majors soon followed.

The vulnerability of the independents was related to the relative absence of concessions elsewhere. The majors, in contrast, could shift production to other fields in the Middle East if Libyan production were restricted. The independents were unwilling to maintain a united bargaining front with the majors against the Libyan government unless lost production was assured by the majors at cost. This, the majors were unwilling to do.[27]

Following this graphic demonstration of the enhanced bargaining power of producer countries, other arrangements were concluded. The oil companies and the OPEC countries of the Persian Gulf concluded the Tehran Agreement of February 1971 and the Mediterranean parties concluded the Tripoli Accord of April 1971, firmly establishing the price-setting prerogatives of the producer countries. The effect was a jump in the posted price which, in certain regions, exceeded $3.00 per barrel, a tremendous increase from the 1969 posted price of $1.80 (the actual selling price was $1.00 to $1.10).

In addition to wresting away the power to set the price of oil, producer countries used their new-found leverage to accelerate demands for full control over their resources. Within two years, by 1973, virtually every country in the Middle East had concluded agreements with the oil companies calling for 25 percent participation. The exceptions were Algeria, Iraq, and Libya, which nationalized the foreign oil companies operating in their countries, and Iran, where the government finally acquired full control of its operations in 1973, although the oil sector had been nationalized since 1952.[28]

The OPEC countries were now in a position to determine production as well as pricing policy, reversing the previously existing relationship between oil company and producer. Combined with changes in German, French, and Dutch energy patterns over the previous decade, these events precipitated a reassessment of national energy strategies.

NATIONAL ENERGY POLICIES RECONSIDERED

In spite of West German efforts to slow the transition from coal to oil, energy imported into the country rose from 6 percent of total energy consumption in 1957 to 55 percent by 1972; in France, the growing dependence on imported energy was equally dramatic—from 38 percent in 1960 to 66.6 percent in 1970. As long as oil had remained inexpensive, abundant, and accessible, energy dependence was not perceived as a serious problem. With the transformation of the world energy market in the early 1970s, however, these assumptions quickly became obsolete.

Before these developments, West German government officials had shown little inclination to tamper with their domestic oil sector, despite the dominant position enjoyed by the international majors in this market. Collectively, the international majors owned 75 percent of the refining facilities in the Federal Republic and controlled over 50 percent of the distribution outlets.[29] Equal access was granted to all companies, domestic or foreign; and even in instances where a major took over a German oil company, the government remained strictly neutral. In 1966, for example, there was a takeover of Deutsche Erdoel by Texaco; and during the same period, Mobil increased its participation in the distribution chain Aral from 11 percent to 29 percent, while Shell and Esso had gained control of the German oil company Elwerath.[30]

By the late 1960s, however, the government was becoming much less sanguine about the predominance of the foreign companies in the oil market. These concerns initially were due less to OPEC, which hadn't yet begun to flex its muscles, than to three other factors. First, the Western Hemisphere (United States, Canada, Venezuela) was no longer in a position to serve as a reserve for Western Europe in case of supply difficulties in the Middle East and Northern Africa. (During the 1956 Arab-Israeli War, the United States had supplied oil to Western Europe until the Suez Canal was reopened and the regular supply restored; during the 1967 war, the United States again offered aid, but the supply situation was such that the Europeans didn't need it.) Second, as the United States was fast becoming the largest consumer of Middle Eastern oil, it was also emerging as a powerful competitor for oil in that region. Third, as a consequence, U.S.-based international majors were becoming subject to American government pressure during periods of crisis.

First indications of the growing West German concern appeared toward the end of 1968, as the French oil company CFP made a bid for the Dresdener Bank's minority holdings in Gelsenberg, the largest remaining German-controlled oil company and the only one with worthwhile overseas concessions. Just before the deal was concluded, the federal government intervened. Forbidding the sale of Dresdener's holdings to foreign interests, the government arranged for the purchase of Gelsenberg (Dresdener's shares plus those owned by the Deutsche Bank) by the public utility RWE.[31] This was followed by a second initiative in February 1969: the establishment of a national oil organization called Deminex (*Deutsche Erdoelversorgungsgesellschaft*).

Composed of eight German companies, Deminex was a government-sponsored effort to strengthen the crude oil base of German oil companies either through exploration, acquiring production rights in proven fields overseas, by participation in the exploration ventures of other groups, or by long-term purchasing arrangements. German oil companies, with the possible exception of Gelsenberg, had virtually no directly-owned crude oil. During periods of surplus, this created no problem since oil could be purchased on the spot market at bargain prices. But in times of tight oil supply, which were developing in the late 1960s because of the closing of the Suez Canal and a subsequent temporary tanker shortage, these oil companies had to rely on higher-priced crude purchased from those controlling production—primarily the international majors.

Finally, by 1973, proposals were in the works for the creation of a strong national oil company to operate internationally. Energy officials in Bonn had drawn certain conclusions from recent events in the Middle East. They believed that producer countries were no longer content simply to increase oil revenues; rather, these countries wanted to use their wealth to further economic development. They were, therefore, interested in finding potential partners able to help in the industrialization of their countries. The international majors were less suited and less willing to engage in the type of state-trading arrangements preferred by the producer countries. With Veba—a large, German-owned energy concern in which the government already held 40 percent interest—to serve as the nucleus, a state company would be able to take advantage of changes in the international market and provide a negotiating partner able to accommodate the interests of producing countries and at the same time profit from new access to crude oil.

Thus, the early 1970s contained the seeds of a new era in German energy policy. Although still in the initial stages, the scope of government energy policy had enlarged appreciably. No longer restricted to the coal sector, industrial reorganization in the oil sector was impending. In addition, the environmental ramifications of energy policy choices were becoming more politically salient. Finally, as we will see later, nuclear energy was on the threshold of large-scale application and this would bring greater government involvement in development and regulation.

Recent changes in the world energy market also led to a reevaluation of energy strategies in the other two countries of this study, although the resulting initiatives were considerably more modest than in Germany. For Dutch officials, the unsettling developments in the Middle East combined with growing fears that gas supplies might be exhausted sooner than anticipated. The consequence was a decision in 1972 not to conclude any new agreements for the export of natural gas and, in order to restrict consumption domestically, to increase its price. Along with the hoped-for effect on conservation, the government decision to allow the price of gas to follow that of oil also meant higher profits without increased costs. After long and difficult negotiations, the state pushed through an agreement with Shell and Esso, its two partners in NAM, calling for a larger state share of the profits. Instead of the original 70 percent, the state was to receive 85 percent of the additional profit.

In France, ill-fated efforts continued throughout the 1960s to establish an independent crude oil source. These attempts largely consisted of cultivating special relationships with Arab oil-producing states. Most of the advantages sought proved ephemeral. France's privileged position in Algeria was terminated in November 1969 when Algeria unilaterally raised the price of oil that had been set in the 1965 agreement. By the end of 1970 the price of Algerian oil was aligned with that prevailing on the world market, set at Tripoli by OPEC. Finally, in February 1971, all French oil interests in Algeria were nationalized. In Iraq, although ERAP had obtained a large concession in 1969, the government subsequently demanded higher payments than those contained in the contract, following the discovery of several fields worth developing. As a result, ERAP was purchasing 55 percent of its total crude supply—approximately 35 mt— from American majors by 1973.[32]

Consequently, the French government sought ways to

lessen the country's vulnerability to actions by its oil suppliers. As early as 1971, the following measures were proposed at a meeting of the Council of Ministers:

- Creation of a fund to finance a supplementary effort at prospecting by ERAP both offshore and in black Africa.
- Diversification of supply among the various countries of the Middle East.
- Supplementary stocking of ten million tons, beyond the three months' worth of consumption already imposed by law.
- Encouragement of long-term contracts with producer countries—Iran for CFP, Iraq for ERAP.
- Increasing the French share in petroleum transport.[33] No apparent urgency was attached to these proposals, however, since the Ministry of Finance objected to the large expenditures that such measures would require; it blocked their implementation. Not until the shocks following the 1973–74 energy crisis was there a fundamental reorientation of French and Dutch energy policies.

ENERGY CRISES AND THE OPEC CARTEL

On October 6, 1973, war broke out in the Middle East, with Egypt and Syria opposing Israel. The effects of the war were worldwide, as OPEC actions over the following months acted to transform the world energy market.

Of most immediate impact was the decision taken by the Arab members of OPEC (OAPEC) on October 17 to cut oil production and limit exports on the basis of importing countries' support for Israel. Initial production cuts were to be at least 5 percent of the previous month's production, to be followed by a further 5 percent cut each subsequent month "until Israeli withdrawal is completed and the legal rights of the Palestinian people are restored."[34] Because of their open support for Israel, the United States and the Netherlands were to be totally embargoed.

In March 1974, the embargo was lifted and oil production quickly rose to pre-embargo levels, but a precedent had been

set that has haunted government officials in the oil importing countries of the West ever since. Concern over the future
use of embargo as a political weapon, however, was not the
only legacy of the 1973–74 energy crisis.

Between October 1973 and January 1974, a succession of
price hikes by OPEC pushed the price of oil from $3.00 to
$11.65 per barrel. Though slower in developing, the effects of
this unanticipated increase were devastating in the advanced industrial economies, as they experienced declining
economic growth, rising unemployment, and higher inflation (see Table 6). Equally important, however, the effects of
this fourfold price rise were not limited to the industrial
democracies. With worldwide demand for oil dropping
sharply as economic recession deepened, the OPEC cartel
was to face its first major challenge.[35]

Because OPEC was a newly formed cartel that relied on
price setting rather than production quotas to control the oil
market, accumulating surpluses threatened an outbreak of
price competition among exporters wishing to maintain
their market share. Predictions of OPEC's collapse prolifer-
ated.[36] Yet, despite such pressures and predictions, OPEC
managed to survive—in no small measure because of the
central position assumed by Saudi Arabia in the cartel. With
a large surplus production capacity, huge reserves, and a
small population that placed comparatively modest demands on oil revenues, the Saudis were able to pursue their
policy objectives with much greater flexibility than most
other OPEC members. For countries such as Indonesia,
Nigeria, Algeria, Ecuador, Iran, and Iraq—states that either
had large populations or populations large in relation to
their oil incomes—policies requiring revenue-reducing actions such as lowering production meant considerable hard-
ship and sacrifice for their development programs. More
similar to Saudi Arabia in their relatively large production
capacity, reserves, and small populations—and hence often
in coalition with them—were countries such as Kuwait and
the United Arab Emirates (UAE).

By the latter part of 1976, pressures were developing

within OPEC—first and foremost from Iran—for a further price increase of 15 percent. Because of their assessment of their long-term interests, the Saudis strongly opposed these efforts. With little need for additional surplus revenues and, at the same time, possessing reserves large enough to sustain oil production far into the future, the Saudi leadership opposed an OPEC pricing policy that it feared would hasten the substitution of alternative energy sources for oil. Unable to resolve the disagreement within OPEC, Saudi Arabia increased production by 3 mbd, thereby forcing the rest of OPEC to compromise during the course of 1977—the price of oil rose only 10 percent. Thus, despite lagging demand and internal tensions between 1974 and 1978, OPEC held together.

There was some slippage in oil prices when the effects of world inflation and the depreciation of the dollar were taken into account (oil prices were denominated in dollars). One writer cited a decline of 15 percent in purchasing power for OPEC, not including a precipitous drop in the value of the dollar in 1978. Overall *revenues*, however, more or less kept pace with inflation during the period. This was the result of higher taxes on foreign oil company operations and the termination of private ownership in the producer countries after 1973.[37]

By 1978, a state of general equilibrium had been brought to the world oil market, in large part because of accelerating oil consumption in the United States, accompanied by its increasing reliance on Middle Eastern oil. Oil consumption had actually declined by 2.3 percent in Western Europe and Japan between 1973 and 1978, but consumption in the United States had increased by 12 percent and imports by 28.5 percent over the same period.[38] Consequently, when about 4 percent of world oil supplies was lost following the collapse of the Shah's government in Iran, there was little spare production to buffer the crisis. Panic buying on the spot markets ensued, sending prices on those spot market transactions skyrocketing.[39] The cohesiveness of the cartel was again brought into question.

Between December 1978 and October 1979, spot market prices jumped from $12.70 to $38 per barrel, with some sales rumored to be as high as $50. To cash in on such a bonanza, many producers shifted more of their sales to the spot market; but more importantly, they used these spot market prices to help determine the price in their long-term contracts.[40] This, in turn, led to a wholesale disintegration of OPEC's existing price structure.

In June 1980, OPEC made an initial attempt to restore some semblance of order to the pricing system, but it was unsuccessful. Rather than agreeing on a unified price structure, members decided to allow prices to range from $32 to $37 per barrel. Saudi Arabia, however, refused to go along, keeping its price at $28. North African oil was selling for as much as $40 to $41 by 1981.

Again, the Saudis' primary concern was that a rapid acceleration of oil prices might threaten the long-term value of its massive oil reserves. The foremost objective of Saudi policy was to reunify OPEC prices at a lower level. Accordingly, they pushed their output to over 10 mbd in 1981. This, combined with plummeting demand in the industrialized world owing to deep economic recession, conservation, and increased non-OPEC output—primarily from the North Sea, Mexico, and the North Slope of Alaska—set the conditions for just such an outcome.

With a growing glut on the international oil market, many instances of competitive price cutting both within and outside OPEC, and predictions of a further decline in world demand, a compromise among OPEC members was reached in October 1981. A unified price structure was restored, with Saudi marker crude set at $34 per barrel. At the same time, Saudi Arabia reduced production from 10 to 8 mbd. In March 1982, the agreement was supplemented by a decision to impose an output ceiling of 17.5 mbd on cartel production.

Pressures on both the price structure and production ceiling continued, however, as various members discounted prices or ignored the output quotas. Among the chief offenders were Iran, Nigeria, Libya, Indonesia, and Venezuela.[41] As a consequence, further price reductions to $29 were adopted at a meeting of OPEC in March 1983. These were followed in October and November 1984 by a lowering of quotas from 17.5 to 16 mbd, with Saudi Arabia absorbing 43 percent of the cut, after Nigeria reduced the price of its light crude by $2 (down to $28), and thereby threatened OPEC's official price structure.

Nigeria lowered its price in response to price cuts for Norwegian and British North Sea oil, a light grade crude similar to Nigeria's. This type of crude oil had been experiencing low demand and spot market prices, because of recent improvements in refining facilities, which allowed the upgrading of the cheaper heavy crude into more valuable light products. This, in turn, had led to demands from light crude producers within OPEC such as the UAE and Nigeria to realign the differentials in the official price structure, light crude traditionally having been priced $3 higher than heavy crude.

All told, what had been labeled the second oil crisis for the industrial democracies also proved the greatest challenge to OPEC to that time—a precipitous drop in OPEC's oil production from approximately 30 mbd in 1980 to 16–17 mbd by November 1984, debilitating revenue shortfalls for all but the most affluent members, lingering instances of cheating, and a bitter armed conflict between the member states of Iran and Iraq.[42] Yet, despite all these difficulties, the cartel, however battered and bruised, had not broken.

Even more to the point, if OPEC is not the force it once was on the international oil market, consumers of the industrialized West can take little solace in this perhaps transitory eclipse. Consider these points:

- For the countries of Western Europe, imported oil still constitutes a large share of energy consumption.
- The Iranian revolution, the Iran-Iraq war, and the possible spillover of these conflicts into the Persian Gulf region indicate the tenuous nature of the current oil glut.
- Over the longer term, the power of the Middle Eastern oil

producers is likely to increase as the market eventually tightens, because approximately two-thirds of the world's present oil reserves are located within OPEC.

In the next chapter, I will examine just how the governments of West Germany, France, and the Netherlands have responded to the series of dramatic changes in the world energy market over the past decade.

3. The Energy Crises of the 1970s

As we saw in the previous chapter, erosion of the international majors' oligopolistic hold on the world oil market led to declining prices through the 1960s. At the time, the preference of energy officials in West Germany, France, and the Netherlands was to allow the international market to determine the shape, content, and direction of national energy policy. The result was a growing dependence on inexpensive, readily available imported oil. Government intervention, when it did occur, had limited aims, such as to protect the German coal sector or to secure French oil supplies.

With the emergence of OPEC as a force on the world energy market by the early 1970s, government officials began to reevaluate the basic assumptions underpinning their existing energy strategies. Only after the events of 1973–74, however, did policymakers fully realize the extent to which the energy market had been transformed. Such a transformation required dramatic responses. To these responses, we now turn.

As we will see in the pages that follow, many of the general characteristics and policy objectives of the three countries were at the outset remarkably similar:

- Each country acknowledged an active central role for government in the formulation and execution of energy policy.

- Energy policy itself was defined much more comprehensively to include activities in virtually all energy sectors; the interactions of these activities were assessed for their effects on future energy patterns; and the implications for preferred political, economic, and environmental outcomes were examined.
- The overriding rationale or policy objective of each country's energy strategy was to reduce dependence on imported oil.
- The rapid expansion of nuclear power was seen as critical to the realization of this objective.

Despite these similarities, significant differences emerged in subsequent years, most noticeably in the area of nuclear policy. In later chapters, I will analyze in detail the respective ability or inability of the French, German, and Dutch governments to implement their nuclear programs. However, in order to appreciate the importance attached by these nations to nuclear power, we must examine its place within the broader framework of each nation's overall energy strategy. That is the task of this chapter.

THE ENERGY CRISIS AND ITS IMMEDIATE AFTERMATH

In West Germany, the immediate effects of the oil producers' cutbacks in production and the boycott of strategically chosen consumer countries were shortfalls of oil supplies over the next months. Compared to October 1973, supplies of crude oil were down 7 percent in November, 12 percent in December, and 13 percent by January. The Federal Republic was hit especially hard in the light fuel oil used for home heating and the gasoline and diesel fuel used for transportation, because it had to import 30 percent of its refined fuel needs. During the same months, imports of refined products fell 8 percent, 21 percent, and 32 percent respectively.[1] The price increase from DM 76 per ton in September 1973 to DM 230 per ton by March 1974 only added to the anxiety and uncertainty stemming from declining oil supplies.[2]

Empowered by hastily-passed legislation, the Law to Secure the Energy Supply (*Energieversorgungsgesetz*), the federal government responded to these events with the imposition of speed limits on November 19, 1973, and a driving ban for the following four Sundays. Additional measures were less specific: the government appealed for energy conservation, created a clearing office to help distribute petroleum products in case of bottlenecks, and initiated an information and reporting system to keep tabs on developments in the oil industry. Calls for stronger measures within the SPD/FDP government coalition were resisted. Left-wing Social Democrats wanted price controls imposed on oil products; the "Jusos," the official group of younger SPD members, even demanded the nationalization of the oil sector.[3]

In addition to taking these ad hoc measures to ameliorate the most immediate dangers of the supply shortage, the government pursued direct negotiations with producer countries in an attempt to secure agreements on future oil deliveries. Under the leadership of Hans Friderichs, the Minister of Economics, an industrial consortium was formed to negotiate industrial projects with Iran in return for oil and gas supplies; but deals guaranteeing oil supplies in return for industrial cooperation were not immediately forthcoming. By fall 1974, a barter deal was concluded with Saudi Arabia in which certain industrial projects were exchanged for the delivery of 12 million tons of oil over a three-year period, but no guarantee against embargo was included in the agreement.[4] These efforts to acquire more secure supplies of oil through barter deals proved less successful than originally hoped for, although negotiations did continue with various producer countries. Subsequent industrial agreements did help in the recycling of petrodollars and in maintaining a favorable balance of payments.

On the whole, the Federal Republic came through the crisis period in fairly good shape. Without price controls, more petroleum products entered the German market than might have otherwise done so; during the first seven months of 1974, the country enjoyed a DM 16 billion balance-of-payments surplus; and the inflation rate remained virtually unchanged, at about 7 percent. But the nation didn't emerge unscathed from the experience. There had been a decline in real GNP in 1974 instead of the 5 percent rate of growth in 1973 and a subsequent doubling of the unemployment rate— 4 percent by the latter part of 1974—thus provoking questions about the exact relationship between economic growth and energy consumption.[5] There was also concern about the future use of the oil weapon following its first effective application.

In France, the oil embargo and price hikes triggered by the Yom Kippur war were initially greeted somewhat nonchalantly by the French government, in spite of the country's high dependence on imported oil. Having been designated as friendly by the Arab oil producers, France was not to suffer any supply restrictions. In sharp contrast to other European countries, such as West Germany, France did virtually nothing to reduce oil consumption.[6] It soon became clear, however, that France would not be untouched by the crisis. One reason was that, despite France's exemption from the oil embargo, oil imports had begun to decline, albeit only 3 percent under the previous year—this in contrast to a decline of 11 percent in German oil imports over the first half of 1974. The decline in French oil imports resulted largely from an informal decision by the oil companies to divert oil from exempted markets to those more affected by the embargo.[7] But more important than the import reduction, although the effects were somewhat slower in manifesting themselves, was the fourfold increase in oil prices, which was beginning to have a devastating impact on France's balance-of-payments position. Whereas 1972 showed a F 1.46 billion surplus, the balance of payments fell to a F 3 billion deficit in 1973 and a F 28.8 billion deficit the following year. Nevertheless, initial responses in France to the energy crisis were limited primarily to attempts to conclude bilateral state-to-state deals with oil producers.

The Netherlands, unlike France, was designated as unfriendly by the Arab oil exporters, and as such, was hit by a total oil embargo. The Dutch government rapidly implemented emergency measures—a ban on Sunday driving; speed limits, initially through request and later by law; lowering of temperatures in public buildings, offices, and factories; replacement of heavy oil by coking coal in steel production; altering methods used in power plants which normally changed over from gas to oil with cold weather; temporary rationing of gasoline; and the like. In retrospect, these measures proved more than adequate. Despite the embargo, stocks of oil stored in the country during the last quarter of 1973 and the first quarter of 1974 were sufficient to cover 110 days requirements, the highest in the European Community—a situation largely attributable to the redistributive activities of the international majors. Yet, although the Netherlands had managed to avoid the more proximate dangers accompanying the energy crisis, the embargo went far to finish undermining the assumptions that had guided Dutch energy policy into the 1970s. It was clear that the international oil market no longer assured the Netherlands of an adequate, comparatively inexpensive energy supply.

Thus, the events of 1973–74 reminded government officials—and impressed the general public—in all three countries that energy had become an integral component of most activities of modern society and that an automatic supply of this energy was no longer a foregone conclusion. Those in positions of responsibility resigned themselves to a complete reconsideration of their nations' energy strategies.

NATIONAL ENERGY STRATEGIES

By the latter part of 1974, oil prices had stabilized, production had returned to normal, and signs of an oil glut even were beginning to appear on the world market. With the most immediate dislocations of the energy crisis having passed, government officials were ready for a fundamental reassessment of their national energy strategies.

The West German minister of economics, Hans Fri-

derichs, wrote in 1974, "An energy policy is one of the main
political tasks today. The supreme responsibility of the state
for a secure, adequate and, in the long term, viable energy
supply which also takes into account the needs of environmental protection, requires an integrated, comprehensive
strategy."[8]

He thus acknowledged a fundamental change in the interpretation of government responsibility in the energy sector. Rather than being limited to the protection of a declining coal sector, government policy would now include the
overall securing of low-cost energy supplies in the short,
medium, and long term, while respecting the needs for
environmental protection. Energy policy was to be viewed
much more comprehensively.

The first significant step toward a comprehensive long-
term energy strategy was the publication of an energy program for the Federal Republic on September 26, 1973.[9] But
the course of events quickly invalidated many of the program's estimates and assumptions. Within days of its publication, the Yom Kippur war had erupted; within weeks the
Arab countries had announced cutbacks in oil production
and an oil embargo; and within months the price of oil had
more than quadrupled. In October 1974, the program was
revised.

Although similar to the original 1973 program, the 1974
revision contained several shifts in emphasis. The most
significant was the new goal of reducing the country's dependence on imported oil; the original program had been
intended to stabilize the proportion of annual oil consumption over the next decade. (For a comparison of the original
program with the first revision, see Tables 7 and 8.)

The revised program was to reduce the share of oil to 44
percent of total energy consumption by 1985, 10 percent less
than projected in the original program. This was to be
achieved in three ways. First, the use of nuclear energy and
natural gas would be accelerated. The installation of 45,000
MW or possibly 50,000 MW production capacity by 1985 was
deemed necessary if nuclear energy was to play its role in

reducing dependence on oil; this would be approximately 40 percent of total electricity production. Natural gas was to assume an 18 percent share of total consumption by 1985, where the 1973 program had called for 15 percent. Second, coal production was to be maintained at the 1973 level of 94 million tons through 1980, rather than reducing coal output to 83 million tons by 1978. And third, greater effort was to be made in the area of energy conservation.[10] The federal government then set out to implement the major elements of this energy program—with varying degrees of success.

The coal sector experienced a short-lived resurgence following the oil embargo; but it soon reverted to its permanent state of crisis. A worldwide recession in the steel industry, combined with stagnating demand for electricity as well as declining energy consumption in general, resulted in lower coal sales, growing stockpiles, increasing losses, and continued government subsidization. In 1974 and 1975, coal consumption had dropped 14 percent below the 1973 level. By December 1977, record stockpiles of coal, exceeding 33 million tons, had accumulated with a surplus production capacity of 15 million tons per year. This translated into losses for Ruhrkohle of DM 400 million in 1977 and government subsidies totaling over DM 8.7 billion between 1974 and 1977—3 billion in 1977 alone.[11] These events, combined with the legal problems encountered in the construction of new coal-fueled power plants, played havoc with government efforts to maintain coal consumption at the level called for in the first revision.

Although construction on a number of coal-burning power plants were said to be affected, the grievances of the coal sector coalesced around the thwarted plans of the Steag utility to expand the capacity of its plant at Voerde from 1400 to 2100 MW. Approved by the government licensing authorities in North Rhine-Westphalia, the decision was appealed by a local citizens' initiative. In summer 1976, the higher court stopped construction on the grounds that it would add to the already high level of air pollution afflicting the area.

The coal interests were especially vocal in their criticism of this ruling since the proposed power plant would have complied with the emission standards announced by the BMI in conjunction with the implementation of the Federal Anti-Emission Act of 1974, in which the maximum permissible concentration of air pollutants—approximately fifty types of particulate matter and thirty gases—had been defined in what was called the "Technical Specification-Air" (*Technische Anleitung-Luft*, or TA-Luft) and were to serve as guidelines for government licensing agencies. The judges, however, interpreted the standards as defined in TA-Luft as offering only orientation points; as an executive directive, the government licensing bodies were bound by these standards but, as TA-Luft was not incorporated in the law as passed by parliament, the courts were not.

In December 1977, a second revision of the energy program was announced. Despite the problems that we have discussed, it called for coal to reassert its key role in German energy supply. Accordingly, the following measures were proposed or subsequently set forth while the plan was being implemented. First, government expenditures of DM 4.1 billion were to be used for the financing of such programs as the Third Power Generation Law and coking coal subsidies.

Second, to eliminate uncertainties and facilitate the construction of new coal-fueled power plants, the Federal Anti-Emission Act was to be revised or amended so as to make the standards contained in TA-Luft legally binding rather than simply an administrative requirement. The manner in which this was to be implemented was not specified; however, the government stipulated that the proposals should give careful consideration to "reconciling the need for environmental protection and the conditions for employment and economic growth." This phrase reflected an interministerial struggle between the Ministry of the Interior, which interpreted the proposals as a weakening of air pollution standards as well as a challenge to its executive prerogatives, and the Economics Ministry, which was feeling pressure from its clientele in the coal sector. Ultimately, the objections raised by Interior were overruled in the cabinet.

As far as the substantive proposals were concerned, two alternatives were being considered: the explicit inclusion of TA- Luft in the Federal Anti-Emission Law, thereby binding the courts to those emission standards in every case, or the adoption of a presumption clause (*Vermutungsklausel*), meaning that if plants observed the TA-Luft standards, it would be presumed, in general, that no harm was being done. To this extent, the courts would be bound, but it would also enable special regional circumstances to be considered.

Third, under strong government pressure in 1980, the coal-mining industry and public utilities concluded an agreement that committed the utilities to gradually increase the use of domestic coal in power generation through 1995. An amendment to the Third Power Generation Law, adding an additional DM 2 billion to the price paid for electricity beginning in 1978, paved the way for this agreement. Finally, a DM 1 billion program was adopted in October 1981 to support the development of coal gasification technologies.

These measures notwithstanding, the coal sector remains a source of concern, despite (or perhaps, in part, because of) large state subsidies for coal. In 1980, subsidies were estimated to be more than DM 6 billion.[12] Production capacity continues to run far ahead of demand. By mid-1983, stockpiles of unsold coal approached 35 mt, an amount representing approximately five months' supply. In response, the government, with the approval of mine management and the unions, adopted a program to reduce production through a series of adjustment shifts—periods during which miners would not mine, although they would still be paid, albeit at lower rates.

Although the primary objective of German energy policy was to reduce the country's dependence on imported oil, the government program acknowledged that the Federal Republic would have to rely on oil imports for a substantial share of its energy supply well into the future. Accordingly, government efforts in the oil sector focused on securing as reliable and low-cost supplies as possible. This meant, among other things, obtaining direct access to crude oil either by state-trading arrangements or independent exploration. The instruments chosen for these tasks were Veba and Deminex. By early 1975, a merger between Veba an Gelsenberg had been completed and Deminex was reorganized. The number of companies participating in Deminex was reduced from eight to four, with Veba receiving a majority share. Accompanying this reorganization was a government commitment of DM 800 million from 1975–80. Also, a major change was undertaken in operating procedures: the companies belonging to the group had first to offer each prospective project to Deminex and only if it was turned down could a company then go on its own.[13] Despite continued government support, Deminex has, as yet, made only a relatively small contribution to German-controlled crude oil production in foreign countries. It produced 2.4 mt in 1981, this out of total imports approaching 84 mt crude (120.7 mt when petroleum products are included).[14]

Aside from Deminex, developments in the German energy market as well have rendered the creation of a national oil company more a source of vexation than a valuable instrument for government policy. Economic recession, warm winters, and modest success in conservation had the consequence of lowering heavy fuel oil consumption. This, in turn, resulted in excess production by oil refineries in the Federal Republic. (Unlike the United States market where refineries are heavily oriented toward the production of gasoline, the German market is such that heavy fuel oil constitutes one of the major products of the refining process.) This situation was exacerbated by several factors. In the early 1970s, the federal government had encouraged refinery construction in order to reduce the amount of refined products that had to be imported into West Germany. The result was excess capacity. Further, the government continued to push for coal consumption by means of the power generating laws.

The trend in the early 1970s to build natural gas fueled power plants also reduced the demand for heavy fuel oil. Finally, nuclear power plants were beginning to come on line. As a result of all this, production was cut back so drastically that the refineries in the Federal Republic were operating at only 50 to 60 percent capacity throughout much of the period between 1975 and 1977.

Under different circumstances, losses from heavy fuel oil sales could have been made up through rises in gasoline and light fuel oil prices. These products still were very much in demand, but the supply was declining because of the overall cutback in refining. (There is a fixed ratio of products produced in the refining process; the ratio can be altered but only with some cost and difficulty.) With a general surplus of oil prevailing in the European oil market, however, independent German importers were able to purchase refined products at bargain prices on the Rotterdam market. In order to remain competitive and retain their customers, the domestic refiners were forced to hold down their prices to levels near those of the independent importers.

All oil companies operating in the German market were affected by sagging demand, refinery over-capacity, and competition from independent importers, but the international majors appeared to be in a much better position to absorb the losses. For one, they enjoyed a certain amount of flexibility because of their international operations. In addition, a large share of those products being imported from Rotterdam came from their refineries. But most important was the internationals' ownership of practically all oil and gas production in the Federal Republic. The shares were Esso, 28 percent; Shell, 28 percent; Texaco, 21 percent; and Mobil, 12 percent. This production, although comparatively small, provided substantial revenues after the sharp price increases in 1974—an estimated DM 1.8 billion by May 1975 alone.[15] Veba, on the other hand, enjoyed none of these advantages. As could perhaps be anticipated, the types of demands made on government were not uniform throughout the industry.

In certain areas, general agreement did exist among all
oil companies. They were quite unified in their demands for
an end to the tax on fuel oil, no additional support for
German coal, and the elimination of competitive distortions
resulting from government reserve regulations. The government required a sixty-five day reserve (ninety day after
October 1976) for all companies refining in the Federal
Republic, whereas the reserves required for independent
importers were substantially less—the consequence being
an estimated DM 6 to 7 per ton price advantage.[16]

Splits over two issues developed between the "haves"—
the German subsidiaries of the international majors owning
domestic oil production—and the "have nots"—Veba, joined
by BP, both of which lacked domestic production. The first
was a windfall profits tax; Veba called for a tax on profits
resulting from domestic oil production in order to reduce
what it perceived to be an unfair competitive advantage for
the majors. The second issue was government regulation of
the domestic oil market. Veba wanted prerogatives like
those enjoyed by national oil companies in most of the other
countries of Western Europe. Veba, as the chosen instrument of government oil policy, demanded that restrictions or
taxes be imposed on imports of refined products in the
Federal Republic. This proposal was not well received in
the Economics ministry. Not only did it directly contradict
German post-war economic canon, but its adoption, in all
likelihood, would have resulted in considerably higher fuel
costs, thereby adding to inflationary pressures. Up to this
time, West Germany had enjoyed relatively low energy costs
compared with most of its European neighbors, a situation
largely attributable to its unrestricted oil market.

The second revision of the energy program provided an
opportunity to respond to these conflicting pressures. The
government, however, restricted itself to the problem of
inequalities in competition stemming from stockpiling requirements. The only concrete proposal was to create a
public corporation to assume the costs of the reserve system,
holding compulsory reserves equal to sixty-five days con-

sumption, while the refineries would be required to hold
reserves for twenty-five production days. The structural
problems in the refining industry were not directly addressed, and the issue of windfall profits tax was avoided
altogether.

As a consequence, a crisis of abundance persisted through
1978, the positive side being the relatively low-cost energy
supplies enjoyed by the German consumer because of the
inexpensive refined products purchased in Rotterdam by
independent importers. These conditions were quickly reversed in 1978–79, however, when the Iranian revolution
disrupted the world oil supply.

With the scramble among consumers for limited supplies
of oil sending the price skyrocketing on the spot market, the
domestic repercussions were soon felt. For the independent
importers, who by this time had acquired 40 percent of the
German market in refined fuels, the developments were
ruinous. Oil supplies, if available at all, could only be purchased on the Rotterdam market at prices well above those
the international majors had to pay for their contracted
purchases. This meant that the independent importers were
no longer able to buy cheap on the spot market and underbid
the German subsidiaries of the majors. Indeed, the international majors, now enjoying a competitive advantage, were
able to drive many of the independents out of the market
and, at the same time, show handsome profits. For the
German consumer, the combination of higher oil prices and
reliance on the spot market for a large share of its refined
products meant considerably greater fuel costs. In 1979, the
price of heating oil more than doubled, making it the most
expensive among countries of the EC. As these higher energy costs passed through the economy, inflationary pressures mounted. Although the Federal Republic's 1979 inflation rate was low compared with that of other countries, half
of it was attributable to oil price increases.

As a consequence of these changing circumstances, the
federal government was faced with a new set of demands. In
the wake of rapidly rising energy costs and reassuring state-

ments from the international majors in the United States that their profits derived primarily from their foreign operations, West Germany being one of their largest markets, consumer groups and organized labor dusted off long-dormant demands for controls to guard against suspected large-scale abuses by the oil companies.

By 1981, however, conditions again reversed: an oil glut on the world market, declining sales of petroleum products domestically, and refining capacity operating at close to the technical minimum (just below 57 percent of capacity from 1981 through 1983), resulted in large losses for many of the oil companies operating in Germany, thereby exacerbating friction between the haves and the have nots.[17]

Thus, in less than eight years, the German oil sector has been characterized by tight supply and a four-fold price hike, a period of stable costs and large surpluses succeeded by rapidly rising prices and restricted supply, followed in turn by stagnating domestic demand and a world oil glut. To date, government initiatives have been little help in coping with the shifting sets of problems, political demands, and interested constituencies that have accompanied each change.

Perhaps in acknowledgement of its ineffectiveness, the government apparently has abandoned its strategy of having a large national oil firm act as a counterweight to the international majors in the German oil market, accepting the costs as well as the benefits of a largely open, unregulated oil market. In 1983, the government announced that it was reducing its stake in Veba from 43.75 to 30 percent, an action preceded in 1978 by an agreement between Veba and BP that, in essence, provided marginally greater domestic refining and distribution to the international majors.[18] More significantly, the agreement transferred majority control of Ruhrgas, the largest natural gas company in West Germany and Europe, to the international companies—this at a time when natural gas was to assume increasing importance in Germany's energy consumption patterns.

Along with nuclear power, growing use of natural gas was to help reduce the Federal Republic's dependence on imported oil. Representing 10 percent of total energy consumption in 1973, natural gas had increased its share to 16.7 percent by 1980. The continued contribution of natural gas toward the achievement of government objectives has not been without problems, however.

In November 1981, a large long-term contract between the Soviet Union and German gas companies was approved by the federal government. By the late 1980s, Soviet deliveries under this agreement would represent around 30 percent of German natural gas supply—approximately 5 to 6 percent of overall energy consumption, an amount sufficient to create serious dislocations if withheld. Accordingly, while discounting the likelihood of any interruptions, the government has initiated measures to increase storage capacity. Despite these precautions, relations between West Germany and its most important ally suffered considerably as the Reagan administration unsuccessfully pressed the German government to cancel its agreement to help with the construction of the Trans-Siberian gas pipeline.

The final area to receive attention from West German energy officials was conservation. Although conservation was mentioned in previous versions of the energy program, it was not until the second revision in December 1977 that energy conservation was given formal priority—priority in governmental statements, position within the written program, and space devoted to conservation. While the proposed measures were unassailable because no responsible group could oppose the elimination of waste, the program nevertheless encountered certain unanticipated problems.

The most important elements of the program related to the provision of DM 4.35 billion to encourage energy conserving investments in existing buildings, with funds to be provided by both the federal and state or regional (Laender) governments. But major objections were raised by several CDU-governed Laender. At issue was budgetary competence: the federal/Laender programs were seen as a threat to the Laender parliaments. One grievance concerned the proportion of the funds; the federal government had specified a fifty/fifty federal/Laender split. Another disputed the manner in which those funds were to be used; the CDU-governed Laender demanded that they be untied. After a long series of negotiations extending over a period of months, the compromise finally struck called for half of the DM 4.35 billion to be provided by the federal government and half by the Laender, with DM 2.34 billion of that to be administered as direct subsidies and DM 2.01 billion to be used as compensation for a short-fall in tax revenues resulting from the alternative tax write-offs.

Subsequent efforts to supplement the conservation measures outlined in the second revision avoided similar federal and state confrontations; but the debate over conservation continued within the governing coalition. The major point of contention was whether conservation should be compelled by regulation or induced through market incentives. Advocating compulsion was Research Minister Hauff (SPD), who floated such proposals as prohibiting the use of heating oil in new buildings, cancelling all motor sports events, and reintroducing car-free Sundays and speed limits on the autobahns—an issue that has elicited more controversy and discussion over the years than all other proposals combined. Economics Minister Lambsdorf (FDP) was the primary advocate of inducing conservation, placing emphasis on tax incentives and the promotion of greater public awareness. In May 1979, the cabinet adopted a package of energy conservation measures which, although containing elements of both approaches, appeared to be weighted toward inducement. There was no general imposition of speed limits or restrictions such as emergency gasoline rationing, but there were regulations to improve heat savings in government buildings and public housing, plus enforcement of speed limits for government-owned cars; higher insulation standards for new construction; gas conservation as a mandatory part of driving instruction; more car pools with insurance and tax incentives to encourage their use; and public education programs. This general orientation was reaffirmed in the government's Third Revision of November 1981.[19]

When the more conservative CDU/CSU replaced the SPD as coalition partner of the FDP, the change in government only served to reinforce the preference for induced conservation through market incentives.

On balance, in the decade since the 1973–74 energy crisis, West Germany's overall energy policy has enjoyed considerable success: between 1973 and 1983, oil's share of primary energy consumption has dropped from 55 to approximately 45 percent; efforts in the coal and natural gas sectors have somewhat diversified the country's sources of energy; some degree of geographical diversification of oil supplies has taken place, the North Sea moving ahead of Saudi Arabia as the single largest supplier in 1982; and domestic measures such as stockpiling and crisis management mechanisms and international arrangements like those within the International Energy Agency have been established to respond to supply interruptions.

Nevertheless, as one of the largest unrestricted oil markets in the world, the West German economy continues to be extremely sensitive to changes in the price of oil, as the economic figures in Table 8 graphically illustrate. In addition, the Federal Republic remains vulnerable to supply interruptions. Finally, a significant share of the reductions in oil consumption achieved recently has owed more to economic slowdown than to genuine conservation—approximately three-fifths of the 11.4 percent decline in energy consumption between 1979 and 1982 by the calculations of an official in the Economics Ministry.[20] Accordingly, the expansion of nuclear power has remained a top priority for high government officials throughout the preceding decade.

THE ENERGY CRISIS AND FRANCE

In the period 1970–74, French energy policy underwent a significant reorientation in response to fundamental changes in the world energy market. In the midst of the energy crisis, a hurriedly revised energy program was announced by the Messmer government in March 1974. It called for the implementation of certain conservation measures, a stop in the decline of French coal production, some increase in the import of coal and natural gas, and a rapid acceleration of the French nuclear program. Rather than accepting the continued rapid rise in oil imports and the political and economic problems accompanying them, the program attempted anew to reassert state control over the pattern, as well as the volume, of domestic energy consumption.

By early 1975, order had more or less returned to the world markets. Under these less turbulent conditions, a general reassessment of French energy policy was undertaken within the framework of the Conseil Central de Planification under the chairmanship of President Giscard d'Estaing. Although the program announced in February 1975 did not diverge dramatically from the one formulated at the height of the energy crisis, it laid out the overarching principles, as well as specific targets, that were to guide French energy policy over the next decade.

At the heart of the program was the imperative of reducing France's dependence on foreign oil. This was to be accomplished in two ways: diversification of the energy supply, both in terms of alternative energy sources to replace oil and shares of the domestic market supplied by oil producers; and a reduction in overall energy consumption through conservation, building on initiatives taken earlier such as speed limits, limits on times for street display window lighting, discontinuation of favorable rates for high electrical consumption, tax on certain petroleum products such as gasoline, and tax on gas-guzzling cars.

Without conservation, the government calculated, total energy consumption would be 280–85 million tons petroleum equivalent (mtpe) by 1985, whereas the government target was 240 mtpe. (For a quantitative breakdown of the government program by energy sector, see Table 9.) To achieve a savings of up to 45 mtpe, French energy officials began to erect an impressive array of conservation measures

to supplement the provisions made in the immediate aftermath of the energy crisis:

- The state set ceilings on the consumption of heavy fuel oil
  by large industrial consumers, with special fines for exceeding these ceilings.
- Ceilings on the total purchases of imported petroleum and
  petroleum products were imposed; the Council of Ministers specified a ceiling of F 51 billion in 1976, F 55 billion
  in 1977, and F 58 billion in 1978.
- Based on studies of potential energy savings in various
  industrial sectors, *accords sectoriels* were concluded between the state and those industrial sectors that designed
  special energy saving programs. Subsidies and tax pref-
  erences, as well as regulations, were offered as induce-
  ments.
- Quotas were established for sellers of heating oil; those
  who exceeded their quota were either fined or had their
  quota reduced.
- A special tax of 2–3 percent of energy costs on industrial
  concerns consuming more than 15 mtce per year was
  imposed, with plants whose yearly sales were under F 100
  million exempted. Enterprises investing in energy conservation were to be either partially or fully freed from
  the tax.

French officials enjoyed considerable success in their efforts to restrict the growth of energy consumption in a
country already ranking high among advanced industrial
states in energy efficiency: energy savings rose from an
estimated 12 mtpe in 1975 to 24 mtpe in 1980. What success
France has enjoyed in conservation has been due, in part, to
the absence of a major impediment to the implementation of
compulsory conservation measures often encountered in
other major industrial democracies—that of parliamentary
consent. Many of the directives on conservation were issued
as government "*décrets*," thereby circumventing any need
for parliamentary approval; the remainder have been pro-
mulgated in the form of government "*arrêtées*,"—decisions

taken by administrative authorities based on broad, over-arching laws already on the books.

Nevertheless, conflict has not been absent from conservation issues in France. The state agency responsible for proposing and promoting energy conservation (*Agence pour les Economies d'Energie*) had little political clout of its own; only through the Ministry of Industry, which had tutelage over the conservation agency, or government councils headed by the President, could measures regulating energy consumption be implemented. These bodies were subject to pressures from powerful state agencies such as EDF and state oil and gas enterprises that often were more interested in promoting their own particular product than in overall energy conservation.

Despite opposition, conservation efforts continued. In the same year, 1975, the government revised its energy policy objectives for 1990, projecting savings of 60 mtpe, accompanied by further measures to encourage conservation.[21] In 1981, a Socialist government came into power with a strong commitment to energy conservation, a commitment demonstrated by the single largest percentage increase in the energy budget for 1982—59 percent.

Attempts to reduce dependence on imported oil through diversification, on the other hand, have met with somewhat mixed results. The objective articulated in the February 1975 program, that no foreign oil producer should supply more than 15 percent of the domestic petroleum market, has been largely ignored as Saudi Arabia continues to supply well over a third of France's oil. This situation has been due partly to the costs entailed in diversifying supply. Refineries constructed to use certain grades of crude oil would sometimes require sizable investments to accommodate different crudes from other countries. Further, alternative supplies have proved unreliable. Iranian supplies were lost to the revolution and then Iraqi supplies were cut off by the Iran-Iraq war. Oil from Mexico and Venezuela has filled some of the gap, but Saudi Arabia has been the major substitute supplier. Attempts to provide

French oil companies—CFP and Elf-Aquitane—with new
resources through intensified oil exploration off the coast of
Brittany have yielded few results as yet.[22] Efforts begun
under President de Gaulle to foster special relationships
between France and the Arab-Islamic world have continued and been intensified.

In the wake of the 1973–74 energy crisis, the French
government refused to join the International Energy
Agency, partly because of the confrontational connotations
associated with the IEA at its creation. In addition, France
initiated the abortive North- South dialogue, the Conference
on International Economic Cooperation—a forum favored by
the countries of OPEC and oil-consuming developing countries for discussion of energy problems. The conference discussed topics within the broader context of development as
articulated in the demands for a "New International Economic Order." Before Mitterand came into office, French
Middle-East policy had shown a distinct pro-Arab tilt; and
extensive economic ties between French industry and several Moslem states have continued. In pre-revolutionary
Iran and in Saudi Arabia, petrochemical plants and cement
factories have been built; nuclear technology has been ex-
ported to Iraq, Iran, and Pakistan; and sizable amounts of
arms have been sold to Iraq, Pakistan, and Saudi Arabia.
Whether these diplomatic and economic ties constitute some
degree of real security in energy supply, however, remains a
question.[23]

In the gas sector, contracts for the delivery of natural gas
have been concluded with the Netherlands, Algeria, the
Soviet Union, and North Sea producers with an eye to
increasing gas consumption into the 1980s, although these
efforts have not been without their vexations. For example,
during the second oil crisis, the Algerian company Sonatrach demanded a price increase for gas supplied through an
existing contract. The dispute was finally settled by the
Mitterand government, agreeing to a price well above the
world level. Another controversy was with the Reagan administration over the purchase of gas from the Soviet pipe-

line and the associated issue of technology transfer to the
Soviet Union.[24]

In the 1975 program, the newer alternative energy
sources such as solar and bioconversion were to play only a
marginal role in diversification, supplying only 1 percent of
French energy needs for 1985 and 5 percent by the year
2000. Under the Socialists, research funding was increased
considerably, but important contributions of these sources to
the energy balance were still far in the future.

Finally, with French coal production in decline, initiatives were undertaken in the 1970s to increase coal imports,
primarily from the United States and South Africa. When
the Socialists came into office, however, they initiated plans
to halt the decline in domestic coal production and even to
increase it in the future—from 20 mt per year up to 30 mt.
But by 1983, a reappraisal of this policy was underway as
losses for CDF in 1982 of $86 million had increased ten-fold
over the previous year's. In 1984, the government decided to
cut national coal production to 11 mt by 1988 and, in doing
so, halve the CDF workforce of 56,000, despite strong opposition from the trade unions.[25]

Thus, France has made considerable progress toward a
reduction in energy dependence in several areas since the
1973–74 energy crisis. Nevertheless, the economic impact of
the 1979–80 crisis demonstrated the need for further cutbacks in oil consumption. As illustrated in Table 6, economic
growth slowed dramatically in 1980, inflation as well as
unemployment rates rose, and the balance of payments
moved from a $1.5 billion surplus in 1979 to an estimated
deficit of $4 billion in 1980.[26] In addition, the strengthening
of the dollar following the second crisis put even further
pressure on France's balance of trade; despite a decline in
the price of crude oil in dollars, France paid what approxi-
mated a 70 percent increase in the price of oil between 1980
and 1982.[27]

To achieve further cutbacks, the government has adopted
a policy designed to reduce the share of imported oil in
overall energy consumption to 30 percent by 1990, down

from 66 percent in 1973 and 53.2 percent in 1980. The key to further progress toward this goal has been, and remains, the rapid expansion of nuclear power.

THE ENERGY PROBLEM IN THE NETHERLANDS

In fall 1974, the Dutch Minister of Economic Affairs, Rudi F.M. Lubbers, submitted a White Paper on energy policy to parliament. The government at the time was a coalition of five parties. The parties and their percentages of representation were the PvdA (Labor), 27.3 percent; PPR (Radicals), 4.8 percent; D'66 (Democrats 1966), 4.2 percent; KVP (Catholic Peoples Party), 17.7 percent; and ARP (Anti-Revolutionary Party), 8.8 percent. Ten cabinet ministers came from the PvdA, PPR, and D'66, six from the two confessional parties.

Representing a significant departure from the past orientation of Dutch energy policy, the White Paper stated:

> This paper sets forth the various aspects of energy policy in their interrelationships. The basic assumption is that energy sources can and must be interchangeable and that energy policy as such must be integrated with socio-economic policy and attuned to other elements of government policy, including those concerning the environment. International contexts also play a major part.
>
> The paper thus aims at an integrated approach. It is intended to provide the impulse for policy for the next ten years and to be the starting point for discussions on the basic policies to be selected . . .
>
> The traditional role of the government in energy administration will have to be increased. There are new duties ahead for the government both on the demand side (limitation of the growth of energy consumption) and on the supply side (the widening of supplies by volume and variety). This can be done not only by promoting and channelling political orientation re-

garding what is desirable but also by taking stimulating or retarding action in certain cases. It is essential that in other cases the authorities themselves will have to perform certain duties.[28]

Substantively, the White Paper made specific proposals covering a broad spectrum of energy policy concerns—from a slowdown in the depletion rate of natural gas reserves, through the promotion of alternative energy supplies such as nuclear power, coal, and new sources, to energy conservation.

Conceptually, the White Paper represented a blueprint for a future energy plan much different from the government approach to energy policy that had prevailed in the Netherlands throughout much of the post-war period. Rather than allowing the marketplace to determine the country's energy patterns, significant government intervention was foreseen across a broad range of issues. In addition to expanding governmental activities relating directly to conservation and natural gas policy, the White Paper called for greater government responsibility in the electricity generating sector. Up to this time, electrical power production policy had been formulated solely by SEP, the central organization representing fourteen publicly owned companies at the provincial and municipal levels, although, according to certain observers, the effect of public ownership had been minimal.[29] For example, SEP was responsible for a binding nine-year electricity plan for the construction of power plants, a plan not subject to anyone else's approval. The White Paper proposed that the electricity plan be reviewed by the Ministry of Economic Affairs—which would provide some measure of control by parliament—and that a state monopoly be created for the generation of electricity with nuclear power.

Further, rather than focusing exclusively on economic and market criteria, the environmental and social implications of various energy technologies were acknowledged as important considerations in future energy policy choices.

Finally, rather than reflecting a preoccupation with immediate energy concerns—the Netherlands, after all, had just become a net energy exporter—future energy production and consumption patterns in the Netherlands were a major concern. Fears that domestic gas supplies would be exhausted by the end of the century tempered considerably any optimism about the nation's long-term energy outlook. In execution, then, the central tenet of the government program was the extension of domestic gas supplies through energy conservation, development of nuclear energy, and a combination of policies directed at the gas sector.

In its gas policy, the government has undertaken initiatives in several areas relating to gas policy subsequent to publication of the White Paper in 1974. In an effort to reduce domestic gas consumption, the government decided that agreements for deliveries to electrical utilities or industry for purposes of heating would not be renewed. As the Economics Ministry explained, "We want to ensure that we have gas available, chiefly for domestic heating purposes and higher grade and efficient industrial application until the year 2000. After that gas will be restricted to domestic heating purposes." More recently, however, this policy has been relaxed somewhat as inland sales and exports dropped, causing painful cuts in government revenues by 1982–83. More on this below.[30]

To contribute to the diversification of Dutch energy supplies, as well as to prolong the life of domestic reserves, the government has actively pursued a policy of importing natural gas. By 1977, Gasunie had contracted with Norway for the importation of 55,000 million cubic meters over twenty years; and in 1979 an agreement was reached with Algeria on the purchase of 112,000 million cubic meters in the form of liquefied natural gas (LNG), deliveries to begin in 1983. Combined, imports from Norway and Algeria would cover nearly 20 percent of domestic consumption after 1983, a share that would increase if additional import contracts were concluded.

The import agreement with Algeria, already in doubt

because of demands by the state-owned company Sonatrach to renegotiate the price, was effectively canceled as a consequence of the decision by Sonatrach not to build its planned gas liquefication plant during the five-year plan scheduled to end in 1984, although the possibility was held out that an alternative supply contract covering either pipeline deliveries or a later LNG project might be offered to the Netherlands, but at a later date.[31] As for the agreement with Norway, Gasunie had been negotiating for further imports. Provisional agreement for the purchase of Nigerian LNG had been made and imports from the Soviet pipeline were being considered, but both were rejected as Gasunie began to pursue a more "selective" and "limited" policy in the wake of declining sales and lower revenues from domestic gas.[32]

A logical correlate of the policy to increase natural gas imports was the decision to limit gas exports; accordingly, no new export contracts have been signed since 1974, no renewals for existing contracts have been given, and current deliveries have not been increased. But because the sale of natural gas had become such an important source of revenue for the Dutch government (see Table 10 in Appendix), it was equally important to assure that a policy designed to decrease gas exports would not result in an immediate decline in those revenues. (Exports were expected to decline considerably after 1978, approaching zero by 1995.)

Domestically, steps were taken in the early 1970s to tighten the link between the price of natural gas and oil prices. To do the same abroad despite recalcitrant partners, the government initiated measures to strengthen its bargaining position. In April 1975 Gasunie, in which the state held a 50 percent interest, was given the monopoly for the distribution and sale of natural gas overseas as well as domestically. That same year, a gas price law was sent to parliament to allow the Minister of Economic Affairs, if he believed that natural gas would be supplied at a price not reflecting its real value, to forbid delivery both within and outside Holland at a price lower than a minimum set by him.

Efforts to renegotiate foreign contracts proved extremely

difficult. Not all contracts with foreign customers had contained a fuel oil clause to make automatic changes in gas prices to match the price of fuel oil; and even when price adjustments were included, there was a considerable time lag. Only after threats of unilateral price rises by parliament and an announcement by the Economics Minister that "decisions have been taken and funds set aside" to enable a cut-off of gas exports was an agreement finally reached in fall 1980.

At the time, contracts were concluded with German, Italian, Belgian, and French companies raising the average price of gas by 14 percent, bringing it into line with the price of low-sulfur heating oil. The new contracts tightened the indexing of gas prices to heating oil prices; a future rise in the price of heating oil will add 95 percent of the increase to the price of gas, rather than the old 80 percent. Further, the length of time between price adjustments was shortened to five months rather than the ten months provided in some earlier contracts.[33]

As in the energy strategies of most other Western industrialized countries in the years immediately following the energy crisis, energy conservation in the Netherlands received considerably less emphasis than other major elements of the energy program. Aside from the intended conserving impact of domestic natural gas price hikes on gas consumption, initial conservation measures consisted primarily of an efficiency campaign carried through the mass media, in which the consumer was offered practical tips in newspaper and magazine advertisements, television commercials, films shown in movie theaters, and the like. Such initiatives had some effect. Between 1968 and 1973, the growth in overall energy consumption had increased at an annual rate of 9.3 percent whereas it rose by only 0.7 percent per year in 1973–77. Oil consumption, increasing 9 percent annually before the energy crisis, was reduced to approximately 1.6 percent by 1978; in electricity, consumption rose only 2.2 percent in 1977 compared with an average of 8.4 percent in 1967–77. It is difficult to determine, however, how much of the decline was due to a relatively low level of industrial activity and how much to conservation.[34]

Nevertheless, an impasse developed in the expansion of alternative energy sources; and influential domestic critics of Dutch energy policy began to demand a greater emphasis on conservation. These developments led to a reconsideration of the government's commitment to energy conservation by 1977–78.

Action was delayed by a long change in governments following national elections held in May 1977. Only after months of negotiations was a government finally formed in December 1977. Although the PvdA had been the clear winner, Labor was unable to put together a coalition. The confessional parties, campaigning for the first time as a unified Christian Democratic party, joined with the right-wing liberals (VVD) to form the new government. The table compares the old and new parliaments by number of seats held.

The new Christian Democratic/Liberal cabinet, building on measures initiated by its predecessor, announced a twenty-year conservation program designed to halve the Netherlands' projected oil bill by the end of the century. Included were measures to increase insulation of buildings, to tighten regulations for central heating systems, to conduct a large publicity campaign, and to provide subsidies.[35] The public sector was to provide Fl 12 billion of the estimated Fl 60 billion to finance these conservation measures over the twenty-year period. This broke down into annual expenditures of Fl 600 million to be spent on energy conservation, targets that were actually exceeded in 1980 (Fl 756.2 million) and 1981 (Fl 742.6 million).[36]

On balance, the government has been relatively successful in erecting two of the three pillars that support Dutch energy policy. A gas policy designed to husband indigenous reserves is being implemented; and a renewed commitment to energy conservation, backed up by monetary resources, has begun to show results.[37] Yet, in certain respects, the Netherlands appears only marginally better placed than its less energy-endowed European neighbors, particularly over

	1977	1972
PvdA (Labor)	53	43
CDA (Christian Democratic Appeal)	49	48 (KVP, ARP, CHU)
VVD (Liberals)	28	22
PPR (Radicals)	3	7
CPN (Communist)	2	7
D'66 (Democrats '66)	8	6
Democratic Socialists 1970	1	6
Others	6	9

the longer term. While technically energy independent
through much of the 1970s, the Netherlands had resumed
being a net energy importer by 1982. Oil still takes up a
sizable share of domestic energy consumption; the 1983
share, 43 percent, was only a little under the 1973 level, 47.6
percent, and the proportion is expected to increase to well
over 50 percent by the mid-1980s as natural gas use is cut
back. In any event, natural gas is not easily substitutable for
oil in many areas of use.

We can see, then, that the Dutch economy would not be
immune to disruptions in the world oil market, in spite of its
natural gas. To prepare the nation to meet supply disruptions, domestic measures ranging from the creation of strategic natural gas reserves to the construction of boilers
capable of burning both oil and natural gas have been
introduced. But of equal, if not greater, importance has been
the emphasis of government officials on the need for international collaboration in times of emergency, a need made
all too apparent to Dutch policymakers during the 1973–74
Arab embargo. In what was to have been a total embargo of
the Netherlands, fellow members of the EEC showed little
inclination to share oil supplies. The distress of Dutch officials over this circumstance was reflected in statements
threatening the possible halt of gas exports if the other
countries in the EEC failed to hold to "recognized playing
rules," a reference to the commitment to free trade within

the Community, which included oil. What sharing did take place was organized on an informal basis by the international majors themselves. Whether the member states would have eventually launched a sharing arrangement had the oil companies not acted remains in question.

In the event of future supply interruptions, not only would there be direct effects of an oil shortage but repercussions would also be felt throughout the Dutch economy because of the impact on the port of Rotterdam. Oil and oil products represent about 65 percent of all goods handled there. As a consequence, efforts to secure the third major component of Dutch energy policy, the expansion of nuclear power, has remained top priority for the succession of coalitions that have governed the Netherlands over the past decade.

THE ENERGY RESPONSE OF THE SEVENTIES

Although differences in policy mix, institutional arrangements, and energy resources have distinguished the energy policies of West Germany, France, and the Netherlands, their responses to recent upheavals in the world energy market have shared two central features. First, each has attempted to formulate and implement a comprehensive energy strategy designed to reduce its dependence on imported oil. Such a strategy has signified a greater willingness on the part of government to intervene along a broad range of issues rather than to follow the earlier pattern of relying on the market mechanism to determine energy consumption patterns. Second, each country has been led to a conviction that nuclear power is essential to the success of such a strategy.

In the wake of the energy crisis, nuclear power has been perceived to be one of the few available alternatives to oil. Equally important, government leaders have seen it as a secure, reasonably-priced, environmentally-benign energy source. That such a view was not universally shared was evidenced by growing political opposition to nuclear power throughout Western Europe. As the following chapters on German, French, and Dutch nuclear policy make clear, however, the impact of nuclear opposition on the conduct of government policy has not been uniform.

4. Unraveling Consensus in West Germany, 1973–1977

This chapter looks at the sudden rise of the nuclear power issue to the top of the German political agenda in the mid-1970s. As we saw in the previous chapter, nuclear power was assigned a central role in the comprehensive energy strategy designed to reduce West Germany's dependence on imported oil. The German government's view that the rapid expansion of nuclear power was imperative, however, did not guarantee swift implementation of the nuclear program. A relatively small circle of energy officials, who were primarily sensitive to the traditional energy problems of the Federal Republic, drafted the energy program, but its execution relied on achieving a domestic consensus. With the introduction of several new actors into the decision-making process because of government efforts to approach energy policy comprehensively, such agreement was to become extremely problematic.

As we will see, the addition of elements such as environmental groups, the courts, political parties, Laender governments, organized labor, and industrial interests to the domestic political mix made the problems faced by policymakers much more complex. The consequence was an unraveling of consensus on the key component of the government's energy package.

NUCLEAR POWER AND THE PUBLIC

Before the energy crisis, energy issues had not concerned most citizens in the Federal Republic. Conventional energy policy issues had been managed largely within the Economics Ministry by energy officials collaborating closely with interested parties from industry and labor. Likewise, the development of future energy technologies primarily had been the exclusive preserve of officials in the responsible government ministry (the Federal Ministry of Research and Technology—BMFT or *Bundesministerium fuer Forschung und Technologie*), industrial interests (mainly electronics and chemical firms), and experts within the scientific community.[1] But the relative anonymity and isolation enjoyed by government energy officials ended in the wake of the events of 1973–74.

More than any previous event, the energy crisis raised the consciousness of the general population in the Federal Republic. The pervasive role played by energy in their everyday lives and the dependence of the West German economy on imported oil was forcefully brought home during the winter months. With little domestic production and government regulation, the full force of the OPEC price hike hit the consumers in their pocketbooks. But an even greater impact was the threat of an insufficient supply of heating oil, since fuel oil heats a far larger percentage of homes in Germany than, for example, in the United States. In addition, the automobile-free Sundays and imposed speed limits were instructive for a society whose prosperity and sense of freedom had come to be equated by many with the ownership and unrestricted use of the automobile.

Although, objectively, the country emerged from the crisis in much better shape than most, subjectively, confidence in the continuation of the post-war "economic miracle" may have been momentarily shaken in the face of declining oil supplies, a halt in economic growth, and rising unemployment. But the heightened uncertainty and anxiety stemming from the immediate as well as potential effects of an oil shortage quickly dissipated as the embargo ended and oil production was restored to normal levels. What did remain, however, was an appreciation for the role played by energy in the functioning of a modern economy and the consequences of inadequate supply. Not surprisingly, the audience for the revised version of the government's energy program had broadened considerably by fall 1974.

Although the objectives of energy policy in the first revision remained essentially the same as those in the 1973 program, there was a major shift in emphasis. Rather than simply restricting the growth of dependence on imported oil, the new program emphasized decreasing the degree of dependence—from the 1973 level of 55 percent to 44 percent by 1985. The corollary of this goal was quickening the pace of the development of certain energy sources, and this implied the rapid expansion of nuclear energy, from 1 percent of primary energy consumption in 1973 to 15 percent by 1985. This involved the construction in the Federal Republic of approximately fifty nuclear power plants generating 45,000–50,000 MW of electricity by 1985.

Government efforts in the area of energy research and development had begun to bear fruit by the late 1960s. Through a series of nuclear programs spanning the period from 1956 to 1973, nuclear technology had been brought to a point where it seemed commercially feasible. In 1967 the first commercial orders were placed for two light water reactors (LWR) by German utilities; two years later, three more were ordered; and in 1971, five further orders were placed. By 1973, all ten projects had permits to begin construction, with a number of additional plants planned for the near future. For the longer term, government research and development efforts, especially during the Third (1968–72) and Fourth (1973–76) Nuclear Programs, concentrated on the development of two advanced reactor technologies: the fast breeder reactor (FBR), which held out the hope of an almost inexhaustible energy source by the turn of the century, and the high temperature reactor (HTR) which, in addition to producing electricity, could generate very intense process heat suitable for coal gasification.

Before 1974, public concern over nuclear power had been virtually non-existent, despite the acceleration in nuclear plant construction in the early 1970s. In sharp contrast to the United States, where coordinated anti-nuclear movements had emerged by the late 1960s, the Federal Republic was most notable for the absence of nuclear energy as a political issue. Nothing had prepared government and industry officials for the emotional and broad-based opposition that nuclear energy was to encounter.

The spark that ultimately ignited national opposition to nuclear energy was struck in the tranquil, largely rural and agricultural southwest region of Germany, bordering the upper Rhine. In May 1974 the state (*Land*) government of Baden-Wuerttemberg announced the choice of Wyhl as the site for a four-block nuclear power plant, each block to produce 1300 MW. Public hearings were held that November; and by January 1975, officials had approved construction of the first reactor.

It may be useful at this point to describe the licensing process, as prescribed in the Nuclear Energy Act of 1959. The federal government has primary responsibility through the BMI; but the states (*Laender*) execute the provisions of the law in the course of licensing. A company wishing to build a nuclear power plant must, therefore, initiate the process by submitting an application, along with supporting materials, to the Land government.

The licensing authorities at the Land level then solicit studies from experts and advisory committees to evaluate the safety of the proposed reactor. Simultaneously, the Land government forwards the application documents to the BMI, where they are studied independently by standing advisory committees—primarily the Reactor Safety Commission and the Radiation Protection Commission. In addition to evaluations at both the Land and federal levels, the Land government is required to hold public hearings.

Once public hearings have been held and the recommendations of the advisory commissions have been considered,
the Land government licensing agency either approves or
denies the application. Nuclear plants are licensed in stages,
the most important being the first stage approval (*erste
Teilerrichtungsgenehmigung* or 1. TEG), which approves the
site and allows construction to begin. In the case of approval,
the decision may be appealed in the administrative courts by
any citizen who had lodged formal objections during the
public hearings.

No nuclear facility may be licensed without the consent of
the BMI. The BMI may also require the Land government to
license a nuclear facility; but a license can be denied by the
Land government for reasons relating to jurisdiction in non-
radiological matters such as land use, water, and the like.

At Wyhl, strong local opposition to the construction of the
plant was primarily expressed by ad hoc citizens' initiatives
(*Buergerinitiativen*). Approximately 90,000 signatures of
area citizens objecting to the nuclear power plant had been
gathered. The residents of Wyhl itself (around 2,700), however, were more favorably disposed to the plant because of
the prospect of jobs and the large tax revenues the plant
would provide the town. The feeling was that the Baden-
Wuerttemberg government had cavalierly ignored reservations raised at the public hearings. That is, the hearings had
been a mere formality. With construction on the plant im-
minent, the citizens' initiatives began the only actions that
seemed available to stop the beginning of construction. On
February 18, 1975, approximately 8,000 anti-nuclear demonstrators occupied the Wyhl site—a strategy used successfully in 1974 by German and French citizens' initiatives in
the same upper Rhine region to stop construction of a sulfur
plant in Marckolsheim, a small town located on the French
side of the Rhine.

The government response to this demonstration of civil
disobedience was swift. Two days after the occupation, the
police were ordered to clear the site. The 300 demonstrators
who had set up camp at the site were forcefully expelled by

police using high-pressure water hoses, police dogs, and truncheons.

Coincident with this police action, the Minister President of Baden-Wuerttemberg, Hans Filbinger, attempted to blame the occupation on outside provocateurs, labeling the demonstrators "left-wing extremists." (In fact, a later study commissioned by the BMFT showed that three-quarters of the inhabitants of the region—which voted overwhelmingly CDU, the party headed by Filbinger—were opposed to the nuclear plant, with the most adamant opposition coming from such conservative groups as farmers and vintners.)[2] Officials also attempted to rally public support with dire predictions that lights would go out by the 1980s if construction were not begun immediately on the Wyhl plant.

Within days, however, the citizens' initiatives responded with a massive demonstration, estimated at between 25,000 and 28,000 participants, held near the construction site. At its conclusion, approximately 10,000 people stormed the barriers erected around the site and, despite stiff resistance from the police, were able to reoccupy it.[3]

Because of the considerable attention given this series of events in the national news media—as well as because of the strong opposition within its own constituency in the region—the Baden-Wuerttemberg government decided against further direct confrontations. As the occupation extended through the summer and fall, negotiations eventually resulted in an agreement between the government and contracting utility on the one hand and the citizens' initiatives on the other. It stipulated that, pending a decision by the administrative courts on an appeal of the government's licensing of the Wyhl plant, the nuclear opponents would end their occupation of the site and the contractors would not begin construction. As the atmosphere of confrontation between government and private citizen began to abate in Baden-Wuerttemberg, however, seeds of nuclear controversy were starting to germinate in other areas of the Federal Republic.

Schleswig-Holstein, the northernmost Land in West Ger-

many, was the location of the next confrontation between
government and citizens. In reaction to the licensing of a
nuclear plant near the town of Brokdorf, a series of large
demonstrations were staged in October and November 1976.
They degenerated into pitched battles between the police
and demonstrators. After the administrative courts ordered
a temporary suspension of the construction permit, tensions
between citizen and state eased somewhat. But no sooner
had calm been restored in Schleswig-Holstein than nuclear
opposition erupted at a plant site in the neighboring Land of
Lower Saxony. In March 1977 the most violent clash in the
short history of the environmental movement occurred near
Grohnde as demonstrators attempting to storm the barriers
surrounding the reactor site were repulsed by approximately 4,000 police.[4]

The escalation of violence that marked the series of anti-
nuclear demonstrations between 1975 and 1977 were increasingly seen as counterproductive by the citizens' initiatives. A major concern was the manipulation of mass demonstrations by left-wing groups, leading large segments of
the population to identify anti-nuclear views with left-wing
extremism. The public was already partially traumatized by
left-wing terrorist attacks on major political and economic
institutions in German society, including the kidnapping
and assassination of prominent judicial and business leaders. To avoid identification with such forces, the national
coordinating body of the citizens' initiatives (*Bundesverband
der Buergerinitiativen Umweltschuetz*) declared its intention
to abstain from any further association with large centrally-
directed demonstrations against nuclear power plants. This
decision followed a demonstration on September 26, 1977, at
Kalkar, site of the German fast breeder reactor under construction. The protest was attended by approximately
35,000, with many more reportedly unable to reach Kalkar
because of police controls set up at all access routes. The
event remained peaceful despite efforts by leftist groups to
incite demonstrators to storm the site.

In spite of the violence—or perhaps, in part, because of

it—the anti-nuclear movement played an extremely important role in catapulting the nuclear power issue to the top of the national political agenda. Nevertheless, the *national* salience of this issue was not attributable solely to the activities of the citizens' initiatives.

Local protests occurring before Wyhl had received virtually no national attention. The selection of Wyhl as the location for a nuclear power plant was, in fact, a direct consequence of the Baden-Wuerttemberg government's decision to withdraw its previous choice for the plant site—Breisbach, a town located only a short distance from Wyhl—because of strong local opposition expressed in several demonstrations.

Further, the major objections raised by nuclear opponents initially were parochial or local in nature. Illustrative were the arguments against the Wyhl location:

- Fog from the cooling towers would alter the weather in such a way that many of the major crops of the region (wine, fruit, tobacco) would be damaged.
- The warmer water returned to the Rhine would disturb the river's biological balance, a problem exacerbated by the construction of a nuclear reactor on the French side of the Rhine.
- With large amounts of water to be taken from the Rhine daily (9.6 million cubic meters), much of the vegetation in the area would be damaged by the lowering of the water table.
- Fear of radioactivity escaping from the plant.
- Concern that construction of the power plant in this largely rural, agricultural region would only be the initial stage of large-scale industrialization and urbanization.[5]

The events surrounding the energy crisis focused public attention on plans for coping with the associated problems, most specifically, on the large role of nuclear energy in the government's comprehensive energy program. Once this happened, concern over nuclear energy ceased to be a localized phenomenon. The broader implications of the widespread use of this technology became subject to a public debate that expanded to engage important institutions throughout West German society as well as private citizens and their ad hoc groups. Public discussion was no longer restricted to localized concerns but rather quickly came to include questions about the long-term disposal of radioactive waste; the political, social, and economic ramifications of a "plutonium economy" in which spent fuel is reprocessed and fast breeder reactors are introduced; and the possible consequences for society of foregoing development of nuclear power.

BROADENING THE DEBATE:
THE GOVERNMENT RESPONSE

The events at Wyhl and Brokdorf caught government officials completely by surprise. Equally unanticipated was the resonance that many of the anti-nuclear arguments were beginning to find in the general population. In a study conducted by the Institut fuer Demoskopie Allensbach, citizens were asked how they would cast their ballot, given the opportunity to vote on a plan to construct a nuclear power plant in their area: 35 percent indicated they would approve, 47 percent were against, 18 percent were undecided.[6] Moreover, the study commissioned by the BMFT found that between November 1975 and November 1976, the attitude of citizens with regard to nuclear energy had become increasingly less favorable, as compared with other energy sources.

Attributing this resistance and concern about nuclear energy to misinformation or lack of information, the federal government responded by conducting an extensive campaign to educate the public about nuclear energy. Responsibility for this *Buergerdialog Kernenergie* (dialogue with citizens over nuclear energy) was assumed by the then Federal Minister for Research and Technology, Hans Matthoefer, who wrote: "The federal government's goal in this campaign is to restore the trust of the population in the functioning of the democratic process, especially in that area where much of this trust had been lost—the nuclear energy controversy. On this basis, a broader consensus on the necessity, safety, and tolerable burdens of this new energy source will be attempted. The federal government will make clear that it will push forward in the promotion and development of nuclear energy only within this consensus."[7]

In the first advertisement of the campaign, placed in various newspapers throughout the country, Matthoefer stated: "Nuclear energy in the Federal Republic is not conceivable without a broad base of trust in the population. Many citizens regard nuclear energy with uneasiness. This is understandable. The intensive public discussion over its benefits and risks is welcomed by the federal government. . . . Safety for all citizens has priority over all other interests. The safety regulations of the government are the strictest in the world. Our expenditures on reactor safety are exemplary."[8]

In addition to the ads taken out by the government in the national press, the Buergerdialog was pursued through booklets explaining the actual processes of nuclear power production and public discussions sponsored by the government. These efforts, however, seemed to have little effect, as the clashes between police and anti-nuclear forces increased polarization within the country. The nuclear debate had been broadened to such an extent that government reassurances of safe plant operation no longer addressed the most central issues raised by nuclear opponents.

To counter the arguments of those who were, in essence, questioning the desirability of technological progress itself, the Buergerdialog increasingly took up the theme, "How do we want to live in the future?"

> Those for or against nuclear energy must first of all be familiar with the various alternative energy sources and be able to evaluate them in terms of their present and future importance. In a further step they must understand the macroeconomic relationships of energy supply and which options are associated with which

chances and risks—not only within the national framework of the Federal Republic, but worldwide. Finally, they must become thoroughly familiar with the social benefits and social burdens entailed in the various possible alternatives. We must evaluate all these factors and then decide how we want to live in the future.[9]

And in various interviews given throughout 1976, Matthoefer repeatedly stuck to the theme:

The question about the risks and benefits of nuclear energy cannot be answered outside the more general context of environmental degradation and the debate over growth.[10]

We need economic growth if we want to secure full employment, and we all want qualitative improvements. But even with smaller growth rates, we will need new power production in the coming years. Without nuclear energy, we would expose ourselves to a dangerous dependence on an uncertain supply of oil. A moratorium on nuclear energy would drive the price of oil even higher and increase our dependence on imported energy. . . . The world economic crisis of recent years and, even more, the crisis of the 1930s has demonstrated how rapidly economic decline can lead to a self-perpetuating and even stronger chain reaction of unemployment, falling demand, reduced investment and new unemployment with incalculable political consequences. In this instance, not merely a small portion of luxury and standard of living would be endangered, but rather, the very basis of our democratic state.[11]

In retrospect, this initial government response to the nuclear controversy appeared to have little effect in gaining public support for an expansion of nuclear power. If anything, public sentiment went in just the opposite direction. It did, however, represent a significant change in government's perception of the nuclear controversy; no longer would debate be conducted by dismissing nuclear opponents as left-wing radicals or back-to-nature romantics, with dire predictions of lights going out by the 1980s, or with public reassurances of nuclear reactor safety.

As it developed, this Buergerdialog reflected a dawning recognition of the growing complexity of energy policy. High-ranking public officials understood that new elements had been introduced into the energy debate that required responses if the major components of the government energy program were to be realized.

NUCLEAR POWER AND THE COURTS

The anti-nuclear movement did not achieve an element of legitimacy so rapidly solely by mass demonstrations and appeals to the general public. A parallel and complementary course of action—less obtrusive but undeniably effective in actually influencing the plans of industry and government— was redress through the legal system.

In Baden-Wuerttemberg, where the Wyhl nuclear plant had aroused such emotion, the judges were very circumspect in handling the case. Because of its technical complexity and political sensitivity, traditional administrative court procedures were set aside in favor of more flexible methods. Rather than taking the usual written testimonies of experts, the judges decided on a format similar to a hearing, where experts responded verbally to a catalogue of questions, where additional questions that came up in the course of the proceedings could be posed, and where the more controversial details could be discussed among experts. Following such a format, the judges felt they were in a better position to differentiate between personal opinion and scientific knowledge.[12]

Taking an entire year to consider the case, the court finally announced its long-awaited decision in March 1977. It ruled that the construction permit (first stage approval) should be canceled on the ground that the proposed reactor

was not sufficiently secure against a possible rupture of the
pressurized vessel that housed the reactor core. In addition,
in order to receive a license in the future, the plant would be
required to have an additional containment wall.[13] The
construction stop originally agreed upon for political reasons
was now legally binding on government and industry.

In contrast to the Wyhl decision, which was based mainly
on the hazards posed by a possible nuclear accident, the
decision by the administrative courts in Schleswig-Holstein
focused primarily on the potential problems of nuclear waste
disposal. Questioning whether an immediate start of construction best served the public interest, the administrative
court temporarily suspended the construction permit at
Brokdorf in December 1976. In February 1977, the construction stop was extended until the appeals on the licensing had
been heard in the higher administrative court; the rationale
was the unresolved problems of storage and disposal of
radioactive waste. And in October of that same year, the
higher court ruled that two conditions had to be met before
further construction licenses could be granted by the Schleswig-Holstein government: first, a testable application for
interim storage facilities for spent fuel rods must have been
submitted to the licensing agency; and second, geological
studies to examine the suitability of the site for permanent
storage facilities must have been initiated.

That same month, on the basis of a June 1977 ruling by
the administrative court in Lower Saxony, all construction
on the nuclear plant at Grohnde ceased. The court had
upheld the appeals of a chemical firm and pharmaceutical
firm, which feared contamination of the medical products
they produced because of their close proximity to the nuclear
plant.

The final significant case before the courts at this time
dealt with an appeal of the license granted for the construction of a fast breeder reactor at Kalkar. This case was
distinguished by its focus on the constitutional issue of
executive prerogative in the licensing of a nuclear reactor of
this advanced type. In a letter to those involved in the

litigation on the Kalkar fast breeder project, the chief judge
of the higher administrative court in North Rhine-Westphalia wrote:

> Consider the cumulative environmental problems re-
> sulting from the radioactive waste of many individual
> nuclear power plants and the uncertainty associated
> with the final storage of nuclear waste; [and] the prob-
> lems of military defense in a country with numerous
> nuclear installations. The control of a "plutonium econ-
> omy" in terms of a growing share of investment capital
> devoted to the nuclear sector . . . Because of the possi-
> ble consequences for the Federal Republic in terms of
> national and international interests such develop-
> ments would entail, the question must be examined as
> to the extent to which irrevocable dependencies and
> forces possibly resulting from these developments
> should be subjected to direct parliamentary control and
> the concomitant democratic exchange between political
> parties.[14]

Reflecting a sensitivity to many of the issues being debated during summer 1977, the judge, in essence, was arguing that the Nuclear Energy Act, having been written in
1959, could not have foreseen the long-term, far-reaching
consequences inherent in the application of the fast breeder
technology. His conclusion was that the introduction of a
technology so qualitatively different from its predecessors
required parliamentary sanction rather than simply executive approval. To resolve the question, the judge requested
that the highest court of the Federal Republic, the Constitutional Court, make a ruling on such an interpretation.

We can see that no single pattern emerged from the
rulings of the various administrative courts: construction at
Wyhl was stopped because of the possibility of serious accident; at Brokdorf because of the unresolved problems of
waste disposal; and at Grohnde because of possible radioac-

tive contamination resulting from power plant operations. At Kalkar the fast breeder program was threatened with long delays because of the constitutional question.

The net effect of these court actions, however, was chilling for an industry that only a few years earlier had seemed on the threshold of an era of unprecedented expansion. By the end of 1977, work on three of the thirteen reactors under construction in the Federal Republic had been halted—four, if the three-month stop ordered by the courts for the Muelheim-Kaerlich reactor were included. At plants where courts had not imposed stops, practically all were experiencing delays; of the three plants that were to come on line in 1977, only one actually did. In 1977 only one nuclear power plant was issued a license to begin construction, only one order had been placed (a letter of intent for a 1300 MW plant at Neupotz), and no new projects had been announced. Finally, although construction on the Kalkar project had not been stopped while the Constitutional Court considered the case, the future of the fast breeder program appeared uncertain if approval had to be sought in a parliament where nuclear power in general and the fast breeder reactor in particular had increasingly become the subject of intense internal party conflict.

Thus, in combination with the pressures of environmental groups, the decisions of the courts served to frustrate government efforts to facilitate the implementation of central elements of the energy program. As we will see below, powerful interests in the domestic economy, which for various reasons were intent on the rapid expansion of nuclear energy, took steps to counter this development, thereby adding to the forces tugging on government officials.

INDUSTRY, LABOR, AND THE NUCLEAR DEBATE

In April 1969, with strong encouragement from the federal government, the two major German companies involved in nuclear reactor development—Siemens and AEG—formed the Kraftwerk Union (KWU), a joint subsidiary created to supply the national market as well as challenge the powerful American companies internationally.[15] Once they were able to sever their license ties—Siemens did not renew its license agreement with Westinghouse in 1970 and AEG ended its commitment to General Electric in 1973—the two reactor divisions were consolidated; but by 1974, the year of consolidation, AEG had begun to suffer heavy losses. Problems with a leaky steam pressure pipe in the boiling water technology used by AEG had necessitated changes in the one commercial reactor in operation and six others under construction. With construction delays of up to two years resulting in cost overruns, losses totaled over DM 300 million; and because these contracts had been concluded before consolidation, Siemens was not required to share the losses.

Already in a financially weak position, AEG decided to sell its 50 percent ownership in KWU to Siemens in 1976. Despite the problems that had plagued AEG, however, optimism over the future of KWU abounded within the nuclear industry and government alike. In 1974 and 1975 alone, KWU had received domestic orders for ten nuclear power plants; and with the conclusion of an agreement with Brazil in June 1975, the German company made a spectacular entrance into the world export market—an arena heretofore monopolized by the two large American companies. In the largest commercial transaction in nuclear industry history, Brazilian and West German government and industry officials negotiated an agreement calling for the delivery of two 1300 MW reactors—with an option for six more by 1990—along with the construction of uranium enrichment and reprocessing facilities, for a total cost of DM 12 billion.

The international competitiveness of the West German nuclear industry seemed confirmed when, one year later, the Iranian government ordered two 1300 MW nuclear reactors at a cost of approximately DM 11 billion, with the prospect of more orders in the near future. In 1976, for the first time in its history, KWU broke even and, with these new orders in hand, anticipated profits for 1977. It is not surprising, then, that when the nuclear industry was threatened with

the combined effects of a growing anti-nuclear movement
and the interjection of the administrative courts in the
licensing process, it responded vigorously.

This threat was most tangibly represented in a proposal
introduced by the citizens' initiatives for a moratorium on
nuclear power plant construction. In February 1977, the
nuclear industry launched an intensive lobbying campaign
with the publication of a memorandum written by KWU
outlining the consequences of the proposed moratorium. It
was sent to the President of the Federal Republic, the Chancellor, all cabinet ministers, all members of the Bundestag,
the chairmen and executive committees of the major political parties, officials within the civil service, all members of
the Laender parliaments, important industrial and labor
organizations, and important figures in education and the
media.

The memorandum argued that:
- With a domestic moratorium, 170,000 jobs would be lost
  and, with no further orders from overseas, the job loss
  would reach 260,000.
- The Federal Republic would not be in a position to develop
  the more advanced reactor types—the fast breeder and
  high temperature reactors.
- The highly trained teams of technicians, engineers, and
  scientists would be broken up and, once dissolved, could
  not effectively be reassembled.
- As a consequence of an anticipated energy gap left by a
  moratorium, economic growth would decline, resulting in
  an additional 1.6 million unemployed by 1985.

Subsequent statements by industry officials expanded
some of these points:
- Foreign countries would be reluctant to make any further
  orders since no domestic plants would be available to
  demonstrate the quality of the technology.
- This loss in international competitiveness would lead to
  further loss of jobs and endanger the advanced technology
  that is the basis of Germany's projected export strength—

a serious matter as the country's affluence depends to a large extent on its export sector.[16]

The immediate effect of this memorandum and of the private lobbying effort that accompanied it on those most directly responsible for energy policy was, in all likelihood, minimal. The government, for one, needed little encouragement to push for its own energy policy. But sentiment for a moratorium had been growing within both coalition parties and, if this development were to be checked, organized labor would have to be enlisted as a source of pressure, especially in the case of the SPD.

The appearance of quality of life concerns on the political agenda of the Federal Republic in the early 1970s had not been without effect on organized labor. Included in labor's calls for reform during this period were such issues as humanization of work (*Humanizierung der Arbeit*) and improved living conditions, such as reduced pollution in urban areas. Although there was little question where labor would stand when the choice was unequivocally between job preservation or improved environment, not all choices were so distinct. The sudden emergence of the nuclear controversy presented such an ambiguous issue.

Compared to the total work force found in the German trade union movement, those employed in the nuclear industry represented only a small share. It was, therefore, by no means assured that labor, as such, would oppose a proposed moratorium in view of growing reservations about nuclear energy among large segments of the general population. As a consequence, the overriding priority of those whose jobs depended on a healthier nuclear industry was to mobilize their national organization. Without national union backing, little influence could be exerted on groups within the governing coalition parties to remove the impediments blocking power plant construction.

In the winter of 1976–77, an intense campaign was launched by local union organizations employed in the nuclear sector. These plant workers' councils focused their

lobbying efforts on the leadership of their national unions—
primarily IG Metall (metal workers) and IG Bau, Steine,
Erde (construction). The ultimate intention was to persuade
the powerful umbrella organization of organized labor—the
Federation of German Trade Unions (*Deutscher Gewerks-
chaftsbund*, or DGB)—to come out against a moratorium.
With the decision of IG Bergbau und Energie (representing
the coal miners) to oppose such a moratorium actively, their
prospects were enhanced appreciably.

An alliance of coal and nuclear power would at first
glance appear somewhat anomalous, coal being a potential
beneficiary of any action resulting in restricted nuclear
power expansion. Environmental groups, however, had been
quite indiscriminate in their targets; local citizens' initiatives were instrumental in hindering the construction of
several coal-fueled as well as nuclear power plants. Peter
Reuschenbach, an SPD member of the Bundestag sympathetic to coal interests, estimated that construction on six
coal-fueled power plants, totaling 7,000 MW, with a 1,000
MW plant consuming approximately two million tons of coal
per year, had been blocked because of legal uncertainties.[17]
With the coal sector reverting to its permanent state of crisis
after a short-lived resurgence following the oil embargo (see
Chapter 3), the coal and nuclear industries had enough
common problems to justify an alliance that would counter
the influence of the environmental movement and reduce
the legal ambiguities that had been hindering power plant
construction.

The combined efforts of the local workers' councils within
the nuclear industry and IG Bergbau, however, were apparently having a little impact on the moratorium position of IG
Metall and the DGB. Reflecting a general concern for questions raised by nuclear critics in recent months as well as the
divisive effect of the nuclear controversy within the country,
DGB chairman Heinz-Oskar Vetter declared in March 1977
that the decision for nuclear energy had been taken "without
sufficient political and social discussion and without complete information." He added that nuclear power plants

already under construction should be completed but that a too-rapid expansion would be irresponsible in view of the many objections from citizens and experts.[18]

This position was formalized by the DGB national executive council in a declaration issued April 5, 1977, entitled "Nuclear Energy and Environmental Protection." Citing the linkages between energy, economic growth, maintenance of international competitiveness, the impact of energy production on the environment, and full employment, the statement acknowledged the importance of the Brokdorf occurrences and the associated protest movement in activating the debate on future energy needs and the ways to satisfy them. The statement recognized that no socio-economic formula currently existed that could simultaneously resolve all economic, social, and environmental-health risks. The solution to the energy problem, therefore, could only be found within the framework of political compromise. Since the social system would be endangered if economic growth were foregone, construction must begin immediately on new coal power plants to replace the old and to cover future demand. Finally, although accepting the need for nuclear power plants, the statement called for all reservations to be cleared away before a final decision was made from which there would be no turning back.[19]

The statement went on to specify a set of conditions that the DGB felt were necessary if all reservations alluded to earlier were to be removed:

- The nuclear industry must formulate and submit a safe and economic waste disposal concept, the costs of which were not to be carried by the public sector.
- Before the issuance of a construction permit for the reprocessing plant, no licenses for the construction of new nuclear power plants already under construction were to receive operating licenses, evaluations of the safety and waste disposal situation had to be positive.[20]

This declaration essentially represented a DGB proposal for a moratorium. That is, the use of nuclear power was made contingent on the "solution"—as defined in the above specifications—of the waste disposal problem, but the licensing process that would be required to meet the conditions specified by the DGB would extend over at least a three-year period, during which time no nuclear power plants could receive construction or operating permits.

MORATORIUM AND THE DISPOSAL OF NUCLEAR WASTE

The statement issued by the DGB on nuclear energy clearly demonstrated the competing forces and demands that had begun to coalesce around the energy issue and illustrated the types of choices being required of political and social institutions. However, as the DGB declaration implied, by 1977 the whole spectrum of issues defining the energy debate appeared to have been condensed into the controversy over a moratorium—a controversy that ultimately centered on the problems and uncertainties of nuclear waste disposal.

There is a certain irony connected with the moratorium focus on nuclear waste disposal, since the two groups most opposed to a long delay in nuclear power plant construction—the federal government and the nuclear industry—were primarily responsible for the initial explicit linkage of plant construction to waste disposal.

With an amendment to the Nuclear Energy Law, the nuclear industry was made responsible for the interim storage of spent fuel rods and reprocessing; the state was to assume responsibility for final storage of nuclear waste. Industry's enthusiasm for this division of responsibility, however, soon waned; officials within the BMI, therefore, began in mid-1976 to evaluate various measures that would pressure private industry into completing its plans for a reprocessing center. The government feared that it would be forced to assume the costs of waste management as spent fuel rods began to accumulate from reactors already operating or scheduled to go on line in the near future. Speculation about industry's reason for dragging its feet on plans for the reprocessing plant was that the industry feared reprocessing would not be as lucrative as originally anticipated.

The strategy finally adopted was to suspend nuclear power plant licensing until plans for storage and waste disposal had been formulated. On December 16, 1976, Chancellor Schmidt articulated this linkage, stating that licensing for the construction of further nuclear power plants would depend on whether waste disposal were "adequately guaranteed".[21] The criteria to be used in determining the adequacy of waste disposal, however, were left undefined. It was precisely over this issue that opinions diverged dramatically.

In an interim report on energy policy issued the following March, the government finally defined the prerequisites for further licensing; to be considered adequate:

- A preliminary decision must be taken on the location of a waste disposal center.
- The licensing procedure for the reprocessing plant must be underway through the application for the construction of storage tanks.
- After a study of the safety report on the waste disposal center had been made, the Commissions on Reactor Safety and Radiation Protection—RSK (*Reaktorsicherheitskommission*) and SSK (*Strahlenschutzkommission*)—must make a positive evaluation on the safety requirements for the disposal center.[22]

And with these criteria expected to be met by fall 1977, the largest barrier to further construction delays, from the perspective of the government, would have been eliminated. As the demands formulated by the DGB in April demonstrated, however, support had been building outside government for different sets of criteria to be applied to the further licensing of nuclear plants.

Noticeable for their absence in the energy debate throughout 1975 and 1976 were the political parties, the organizations traditionally viewed as the intermediaries between citizens and government in the West German political process and, as such, legitimators of government policy. Perhaps most indicative of this was a virtual silence during the campaign preceding the national Bundestag elections in fall 1976 on the issue of nuclear power. But by early 1977 both parties in the coalition government, the SPD and FDP, appeared to be making an effort to regain a voice in an issue heretofore dominated by extra-parliamentary groups.

A conference sponsored by the SPD in late April entitled "Energy, Employment, Quality of Life"—the first of its kind by a political party in the Federal Republic—represented a significant step in this direction. The discussions were balanced, well-informed and wide-ranging, touching upon the major issues of controversy in the energy debate. But the conference also illustrated and brought into sharper public focus one of the major problems posed by the energy issue to the SPD—the serious and deep splits within the party over nuclear energy. On the one hand, there was the Chancellor, members of his cabinet, and those identified with the more conservative elements of the SPD—primarily Bundestag deputies from North Rhine-Westphalia closely aligned with labor in general and coal in particular—who emphasized in the discussions the tight linkage between full employment, economic growth, and the unavoidable need for nuclear energy. On the other hand, there were those primarily identified with the left or center-left of the party—Erhard Eppler, a former cabinet minister under Brandt and chairman of the SPD in Baden-Wuerttemberg, being the informal leader of this faction—who stressed the need for a pause in the construction of nuclear power plants for careful evaluation of the alternatives to nuclear energy and the feasibility of a qualitative growth based on energy conservation, preservation of the environment, and, at the same time, creation of jobs.[23]

Its smaller coalition partner, the FDP, was not immune to the sort of divisions developing within the SPD. The FDP cabinet ministers in the federal government—Foreign, Economics, Interior, and Agriculture—and their backers supported Economics Minister Friderichs's energy program, and those identified largely with the left wing of the party pushed for a moratorium.

The first real test of strength in either party took place at the FDP's executive meeting in June at Saarbruecken. By a narrow margin it was decided that the party should call for further requirements for the licensing of new nuclear plants: safe, controllable final storage of highly radioactive waste, technically safe interim storage, and, most significantly, the licensing of a site (first stage approval) for final storage.[24] In other words, those in favor of an extended moratorium had won the day, since the licensing of waste disposal facilities would require several years as opposed to simply initiating steps in the licensing process.

Three months later, a similar showdown occurred at a meeting of the SPD executive committee. A proposal drafted by Research Minister Matthoefer, using the government's previously articulated formula for adequate waste disposal, was narrowly defeated, whereupon a counterproposal drafted by Rudie Arndt in consultation with Erhard Eppler—both identified with the left—was presented. The counterproposal corresponded almost exactly with that of the DGB declaration of April 5. By the smallest of margins, the counterproposal passed. When this vote was taken, however, Chancellor Schmidt and two of his ministers had left to attend a meeting of the emergency group set up after the terrorist kidnapping of Hans-Martin Schleyer, president of the powerful Federation of German Industry.[25]

Although no overwhelming mandate appeared to have developed on either side regarding nuclear policy, support for a moratorium seemed to have gained momentum through summer 1977 with the decisions of the DGB, FDP, and the SPD to push for an extended delay in nuclear plant construction. Even as the executive committee of the SPD passed its resolution, however, there were indications of a shift taking place.

Most importantly, the alliance of coal and nuclear industries that had been forged within organized labor by the chairman of IG Bergbau, Adolph Schmidt, had begun to make its presence felt within the DGB. The months of private lobbying and public demonstrations by the plant workers' councils in the electrical and nuclear industries started to bear fruit when, in September 1977, the membership attending the union congress of IG Metall—the largest and most influential of the German trade unions—joined IG Bergbau—one of the more powerful unions in the Federal Republic—in its opposition to a moratorium. Change within the DGB was inevitable.

At a Bundestag hearing in October 1977, a DGB representative testified that the use of nuclear energy to cover future energy needs was unavoidable and that several negative consequences, especially in the area of employment, would result from permitting further delays in the construction of power plants. This theme had been played up continually in preceding months. For example, in a speech delivered at the IG Bergbau congress, Adolph Schmidt stated, "Currently . . . construction on 10 power plants (whose total investment comes to DM 16 billion) is being hindered by court decisions, delayed permits, and citizens' initiatives . . . If I correctly assess the various relationships, DM 16 billion translates into an approximate 1.5 percent rise in GNP. If construction were to begin on these plants, we would have—according to my estimates—almost 200,000 fewer unemployed."[26]

On November 8, 1977, the executive committee of the DGB made official the reversal of its earlier position, reemphasizing the dangers posed to jobs by further delays in the construction of coal and nuclear plants. Using arguments resembling those of the nuclear industry, the DGB stated that jobs would be lost in construction firms and reactor industries as well as their subcontractors, and that jobs, in addition to factors related to future "quality of life," depended on maintaining Germany's international position in the development of high technology products.[27] For effect, this revised position was announced at a mass rally of approximately 30,000 that was staged by labor in support of coal and nuclear power just days before the SPD was to hold its annual party congress. At this meeting, energy was scheduled to take center stage.

The FDP, also scheduled to hold its party congress in November, had not been exempt from such lobbying following the executive committee's decision in June. Union lobbying had some effect, but most overt were the efforts by the nuclear industry's lobby, Atomforum, to push for a reversal.[28] Its campaign began with the publication of a widely-distributed fifty-page booklet outlining in detail the threatened consequences of an FDP-instigated moratorium. These were similar to those projected earlier in the KWU memorandum: a loss of 200,000 to 250,000 jobs related to the construction of nuclear power plants by 1985, with millions of additional jobs threatened by insufficient production of electricity, an irreversible loss of competitiveness in the world market for the German nuclear industry, and so forth.[29] This document was followed up by more selective lobbying. But having equal or greater impact were initiatives undertaken within the party itself by Economics Minister Friderichs and his eventual successor at the Economics Ministry, Count Lambsdorf, to dissuade colleagues from supporting a moratorium.

These efforts appeared to pay off at the Kiel party congress where, after extremely difficult negotiations, a compromise formula signaled a muted victory for the opponents of a moratorium. Couched in carefully worded phrases, the resolution on energy policy called for nuclear energy only after the exhaustion of all other possibilities—conservation, improved efficiency of conventional power producers, and alternative energy sources, with special attention paid to the interests of the coal sector. In order to cover a shortfall in energy production that was expected to develop after 1985, however, the resolution stipulated that new construction permits should be granted once two conditions were met: safe final and interim storage facilities for nuclear waste, with this condition defined as being met when the government and Bundestag said so; and preliminary positive findings from geological studies confirming the suitability of the site for final storage of radioactive waste.[30]

This decision of the FDP to drop the linkage between new construction and the *licensing* of a waste disposal site, followed within days by the DGB's demand for renewed licensing of nuclear plant construction, set the stage for a battle royal at the SPD congress held in Hamburg from November 15 to 19.

Reflecting the divergent views represented within the SPD and the difficulties impeding the search for a compromise formula to reconcile the various demands, the resolution that finally received the endorsement of the congress attempted to touch all bases. Full employment was accorded the highest priority and, for electricity production, coal was to be favored over all other fuels. Only when additional energy demand could not be met by coal-fueled power plants were new nuclear plants to be licensed; and the prerequisite was to be guaranteed waste disposal. This condition would be satisfied only after the licensing of a waste disposal center, but if a shortfall in energy should develop in the medium term which, for *compelling reasons*, could not be covered by additional coal plants, construction permits for new nuclear reactors would be granted in *exceptional cases* if waste disposal were guaranteed through contractually binding agreements until storage facilities had been constructed (my emphasis).[31]

Thus, moratorium support that had earlier been gathering momentum appeared to be eroding by the latter part of 1977. Both the DGB and FDP had dropped their demands for making new nuclear construction contingent on the licensing of a waste disposal center; and although the new SPD resolution still retained this linkage, the loopholes in its formulation were substantial. "Compelling reasons" or "exceptional cases" were left undefined.

With a modicum of consensus apparently restored through the compromises achieved at both party congresses, the government finally felt able to carry out a long-postponed second revision of its energy program.

A REVISED GOVERNMENT ENERGY PROGRAM

Since the first revision of the energy program in fall 1974, several unanticipated developments had changed the context of domestic energy policy dramatically. There was the swift rise of a powerful opposition to nuclear energy, intervention of the courts in the decision-making process, a growing preoccupation of labor with threats to employment posed by a moratorium, increasing pressures from the nuclear industry for government action, and the divisions developing inside both coalition parties that made government action extremely difficult. At the same time, changes in patterns of energy demand and supply were taking place, as we saw in Chapter 3. The need for a revision of the government's energy program was becoming apparent; but many of these developments also militated against a reformulation of energy policy. Most significantly, only minimal consensus, if any, existed among the disparate interests over the future direction of German energy policy, and this gave rise to conflict over immediate measures, which invariably had longer-term implications. The result was predictable; the second revision, originally scheduled for March or April 1977, was postponed indefinitely.

In its stead, the government decided to publish what was called "Outlines and Key Data for the Revision of the Energy Program" (*Grundlinien und Eckwerte fuer die Fortschreibung des Energieprogramms*) as an interim statement on energy policy. Published by the Chancellory, it documented the issues of greatest concern from the perspective of the Chancellor and his cabinet at that time: "The debate of recent months has demolished the political framework of energy policy. The necessity of increasing energy consumption is being questioned; a drastic reduction in the growth of consumption is being demanded. The question is being expanded to include the necessity of economic growth in general. The discussion, especially concerning nuclear energy, has taken on a moral-political dimension which has led to uncertainty among broad segments of the population."[32]

In responding to these issues, the government emphasized the importance of economic growth, predicting dire outcomes unless growth rates achieved at least 4.5 percent to 1980 and 4 percent through 1985. Among the threats foreseen by the government were the possibility of serious unemployment problems, the inability to guarantee the financing of social security programs, the possible danger to required public investment because of declining government revenues, the inability to solve internal income and distribution problems as well as current structural problems of the economy, the endangering of attempts to alleviate balance of payments deficits and employment problems of important trading partners, and the inability to finance measures protecting the environment. The government then explicitly stated the need for nuclear power to maintain economic growth, declaring that despite the greater use of conservation to improve the ratio between economic growth and energy consumption and the greater use of coal, 30,000 MW of electricity would have to be produced from nuclear energy by 1985.

Aside from these claimed general effects of lower economic growth, the government warned of the loss of 25,000 jobs in the nuclear industry itself, with this number multiplied many times when subcontracting industries were taken into account. There would also be the loss of competitive position from the breakup of specialized teams and setbacks in the development of advanced reactors and of their later commercialization if delays in the construction of nuclear power plants continued. These points corresponded to many of the arguments used by industry in disputing the proposed moratorium.

This general report, then, established government's continued advocacy of swift nuclear expansion despite the arguments of those proposing a moratorium, arguments that were being buttressed by surpluses that had begun to appear in the oil, coal, and electricity production sectors. Although projections of energy consumption were being revised downward—from 555 million tons CE for 1985 in the first revision to 496 million tons CE in the new version, with nuclear power's share going from 45,000/50,000 MW to 30,000 MW— nuclear power was still to represent 13 percent of total consumption by 1985 instead of the first revision's 15 percent.

In December 1977 the government finally announced the long-delayed second revision.[33] Reflecting the controversy that had surrounded the nuclear issue and the hard-won compromises at the party congresses, the government's approach to nuclear energy was much more reserved in its second revision than in the preceding ones; it was to be developed only to the extent "absolutely necessary to secure electricity supply." But:

> Even given priority for the exploitation of other sources [primarily conservation, coal, and lignite] . . . the Federal Government considers the construction of new nuclear plants on a correspondingly restricted scale to be absolutely necessary, especially in a regional context, to meet medium- and long-term requirements in the individual load categories; in view of the high safety standards attained, this is considered justifiable. Furthermore, energy and industrial policy considerations dictate the need for keeping open the nuclear option and new projects will help achieve this.[34]

This formulation was purposely vague and therefore subject to wide interpretation; and noticeable by their absence were the quantitative goals specified in the earlier programs. Only in the appendix to the second revision was the figure of 24,000 MW production for 1985 given and this only in the context of the studies conducted by the research institutes in preparation of the program; it was not to be part of the official government energy program. The government did outline what was to determine "adequate and safe" waste disposal facilities, the prerequisite for any further development of nuclear energy.

Before the publication of the second revision, the government had already done the following. First, it had adopted the evaluations of the Reactor Safety and Radiation Protection Commissions, published in October 1977, which assessed positively the suitability of the proposed waste disposal center at Gorleben. Second, an agency of the government had filed a request with the government of Lower Saxony for approval of preliminary test drillings which, along with further geological tests, were to provide the necessary information on the site. Third, the federal government had reached agreements with other Laender governments on interim storage facilities until the storage tanks at Gorleben were completed.

On the basis of these and other measures, the following approval procedures for nuclear power plants' waste disposal were established:

a. Approval for the construction of new nuclear power plants [first stage approval—*erste Teilerrichtungsgen-ehmigung*] are acceptable from the disposal point of view if the waste is assured—in the case of storage facilities abroad by contracts—until such time as the waste centre has been completed; this includes proof of the availability of interim storage facilities for extended time spans at home and abroad.

In the opinion of the Federal Government these new nuclear power stations should not be granted operating approval until first stage approval for the waste centre has been given or adequate disposal abroad has been assured.

b. Nuclear power plants for which approval has already been given should in the view of the Federal Government be completed. Approval for the operation will however not be given until waste disposal is adequately assured in line with para. 1 of (a) above for the time up to the completion of the waste centre.[35]

POLICY AND QUESTIONS

The second revision, and the events preceding it, graphically demonstrated the types of problems encountered in the implementation of a comprehensive energy strategy as well as the responses such problems elicited.

In earlier pages we have seen the increasing complexity that came to characterize the domestic political arena, with a vast array of actors making competing, often conflicting claims on government. At first, the BMWi and coal interests had been the major participants in the policymaking process, but by 1977 the number had expanded to include environmental groups, the courts, Laender governments, several other federal ministries (such as BMI and BMFT), political parties, organized labor beyond the coal sector, and energy industries (nuclear, coal, oil, and natural gas). Each pursued specific goals which were often incompatible with those of the others. Not only had the number of participants and policy objectives multiplied, but their interactions were greatly amplified by the open, pluralistic nature of the West German political system. Citizens' initiatives and the courts had dramatic effects on the nuclear and coal industries as well as on government energy plans. Repercussions were felt within the major economic and political institutions of the country, which subsequently brought new pressures to bear on government. Government policies also affected developments in energy sectors other than nuclear, which provoked new demands for government action. For example, the coal sector called for more government intervention to counter the effects of low fuel oil prices on coal sales, greater efforts to remove obstacles to coal power plant construction, and less government promotion of natural gas use. Indeed, in its first revision of the energy program, the government had emphasized greater natural gas use to reduce oil consumption and had concluded several long-term agreements, primarily with Iran and Algeria, for the delivery of natural gas into the twenty-first century.

The effect of these conflicts on public officials responsible for German energy policy was to substantially heighten their uncertainty. Among the questions confronting policymakers:

- What are the environmental and political consequences of expanded nuclear production—the physical dangers of radioactivity and the dangers to personal and political freedoms posed by the types of controls and regulations required for such a technology?
- In face of the growing opposition to nuclear power within the country, what would be the political and social consequences of a forced expansion of nuclear energy? Would the present government be voted out of office, or would there arise social unrest resembling civil war?
- Can a country highly dependent on imported oil for its energy supply forego the nuclear option, given the vulnerability of the national economy to an oil embargo or to rapid price hikes?
- What are the economic and social consequences for a society to eschew traditional economic growth patterns in favor of a no-growth or qualitative growth policy? Can it rely primarily on rigorous conservation measures and renewable energy sources? How can it deal with unemployment, increasing social unrest, and demands for redistribution of an economic pie that is no longer expanding?

If public officials were uncertain about what to do, some of the groups they had to deal with had all the certainty that strongly held values or a sense of survival could provide. For environmentalists, the priority of ecological concerns rendered other issues secondary. Their concern for environmental protection meant that their opposition to nuclear power could not be compromised. For the nuclear industry, survival was clearly the motive behind its aggressive advocacy of nuclear power. The industry was not indifferent to public safety, but its perceptions of the dangers were somewhat different from those of nuclear opponents. For organized labor, growing agitation within several powerful trade unions reflected the traditional overriding concern of the labor movement with employment. When jobs appeared threatened, all other considerations became secondary, including the less tangible and more controvertible threats of expanding nuclear power production. Lacking any real consensus on such fundamental questions and facing competing forces not disposed to compromise, the government suffered a virtual paralysis in the implementation of significant elements of its energy program. The initial response of public officials was to delay decisions on energy policy that would exacerbate the divisions within the governing coalition parties as well as in society at large. The political consequences of any policy decision on nuclear energy appeared so uncertain that the government continually postponed issuing a second revision to its energy program. Once this course of inaction no longer seemed feasible, the government opted for a second strategy, one that did not foreclose any options. That is, it hedged its bets. On the basis of the compromises negotiated within the coalition parties, thereby simulating a measure of consensus among labor, industry and political parties, the energy program was amended for the second time.

Thus, the second revision was an attempt to restore consensus to the policymaking process. Conservation was given formal priority; this alienated no one and incorporated the most important element of any environmentalist's energy program. Commitments to conservation, however, were not to be at the expense of developing costly alternative energy technologies. The revision reaffirmed the privileged position of coal, thereby shoring up support within the government's critical constituencies. The plan minimized the future requirements for nuclear energy; but despite the many qualifications and reservations attached to nuclear power, its necessity was still acknowledged by government. As we will see in the next chapter, these broad, vague formulations, retaining virtually all options, failed to revive the political consensus that was required for hard choices.

5. Stalemate in West Germany, 1978–1984

For many government officials and politicians in the Federal Republic of Germany, the second revision of the energy program promised an end to the turmoil and uncertainty that had characterized the past. It provided a framework within which problems of recent years could be worked out in a spirit of accommodation rather than confrontation, enabling the central elements of the government's energy program to be preserved. The signs were propitious: the large, often violent, demonstrations had been abandoned by environmental groups; the various factions within the coalition parties apparently recognized the need for compromise; and both labor and industry seemed satisfied by government pronouncements on coal and nuclear energy. But expectations of progress proved ill-founded, as subsequent events soon demonstrated.

NUCLEAR POWER AND ELECTORAL POLITICS

Conspicuous by its absence throughout the campaign preceding national parliamentary elections in fall 1976 was a discussion of government energy policy. This silence was due, in large part, to agreement among the principal political parties on the central elements of German energy policy. Nevertheless, an increasingly acrimonious controversy over nuclear power had begun to attract considerable public attention. Tensions emerged during 1977, particularly within the two coalition parties, to threaten this general consensus, but the compromises in the revised government energy program of December 1977 appeared to restore a modicum of agreement on energy policy (although the opposition CDU/CSU was critical of government equivocation on the future role of nuclear power). However, the issues that precipitated the divisions within both the SPD and FDP in the course of 1977 had not disappeared—nor had the groups most dissatisfied with the vague government pronouncements on energy policy. Because of their disaffection with the existing political process, environmentalists set out to make nuclear power a major issue in the series of electoral campaigns for representation in Laender parliaments leading up to the Bundestag elections scheduled for October 1980.

GREEN PARTIES AND THE ELECTORAL PROCESS

Continual waffling of the political parties on the moratorium issue throughout 1977, as well as government's unwillingness to take an unequivocating stand on nuclear energy, convinced many environmentalists that the established political parties were more a part of the environmental problem than of its solution. They decided that additional measures were required if the expansion of nuclear power was to be halted.

Until that time, most public opposition to nuclear energy had been organized in loosely-coordinated, ad hoc citizens' initiatives and was pursued through mass demonstrations and court actions. But in March 1977 in France, the *ecologistes* had considerable success in local French elections, receiving up to 15 percent of the vote in several districts. Taking a page from the French, German environmentalists decided to challenge the traditional parties at the ballot box. In early 1978, "Green" parties were formed in Lower Saxony and Hamburg, where Laender elections were scheduled for that June. The Greens performed well enough in these two Laender that environmental parties were organized in each subsequent Land holding elections. By 1980, a national Green party was created to contest the fall Bundestag election, which would determine the composition of the federal government over the next four years.

As Table 11 (Appendix) shows, the Greens achieved varying degrees of electoral success when measured by percentage of votes attracted; however, the numbers fail to reflect the actual impact of the Greens not only in affecting the *outcome* of several elections but also in determining the *content* of debate and the party *positions* in the electoral campaign.

Opposition to nuclear power was the main plank in the Greens' electoral platform, but it was not the only one. Many other themes were struck during the Laender election campaigns, varying somewhat from region to region. Prominent among these issues was the direction of current industrial development, with the Greens recommending the establishment of ecologically benign industries. They attacked problems such as further freeway construction, housing, deforestation, waste disposal, and air and water pollution. They proposed more environmentally oriented planning in transportation and regional and urban development. More generally, they criticized dependence on economic growth and the achievement-oriented society (*Leistungsgesellschaft*).

In an attempt to organize a national party and formulate a program to carry into the federal elections, the Greens extended the scope of their campaign platform far beyond strictly ecological questions. Contained in the program finally adopted by the party were a proposal for the thirty-five hour work week, prohibition of employer lockouts, demands for the breakup of large combines (*Grosskonzerne*) into smaller and more controllable firms to be run by the employees or co-workers (*Mitarbeiter*), liberalization of abortion laws, a call for the dissolution of military blocs in Europe such as NATO and the Warsaw Pact, and unilateral disarmament within the Federal Republic.

Nevertheless, opposition to nuclear power was the core grievance around which the environmental movement had rallied, and the Greens campaigned vigorously against further construction of nuclear power plants, as well as calling for the shutdown of plants then operating. They opposed reprocessing and the development of the fast breeder reactor (FBR). Emphasizing these themes in their initial outings, the Green parties produced minor electoral sensations.

In Lower Saxony and Hamburg, the Greens failed to receive 5 percent of the vote as required by the West German law to gain representation in parliament. What they did do, however, was draw off enough votes from the established parties to bring the FDP (the smallest and, therefore, most vulnerable of the parties) below the 5 percent margin. This cost the Liberals representation in parliament as well as participation in government, for the party had been in coalition with the SPD in Hamburg and the CDU in Lower Saxony. The implications of these election results were not lost on FDP politicians: if the trend continued through to the Bundestag elections, the very existence of the party would be threatened.

The environmentalists had little impact on the electoral outcomes in Hesse, Bavaria, and Berlin, but they influenced the substance of the debate. In Hesse especially, the SPD and FDP waged aggressive campaigns emphasizing their commitment to environmental protection and their reservations about the expansion of nuclear power. This trend continued as attention shifted to northern Germany in spring 1979.

From all outward appearances, little had changed because of the Schleswig-Holstein elections. The CDU was returned to power, the SPD increased its vote by a slight percentage, the FDP remained in parliament although it fell uncomfortably close to the 5 percent cutoff, and the Green party received only 2.4 percent of the vote. Yet, despite this rather small share, the environmentalists had exerted a significant influence on the campaign and its outcome. In all likelihood, they kept the CDU in government because of the votes taken away from the SPD and FDP. But more important, with nuclear power *the* central issue of the campaign, the Green party's unwavering position established the context and starting point for debate. Ever since the Brokdorf demonstrations and the CDU government's role in them, nuclear power had been a hotly debated issue in Schleswig-Holstein. In addition, the controversy over the Gorleben waste disposal center (discussed below) had been intensifying. To top it all off, the nuclear accident at Three Mile Island occurred just one month before election day. As a consequence, both the regional SPD and FDP made every effort to distance themselves from the position of their own national government, with the SPD being especially vehement in its opposition to nuclear power.

Within a span of ten months, the Greens had altered the outcome of several elections, set the tenor and content of certain campaigns, and compelled the established parties to address the issues that most concerned the environmentalists. What they had failed to do up to this point, however, was demonstrate an ability to play anything but a spoiler's role, that is, to be more than a protest vote. This changed as the 5 percent threshold was surmounted in Bremen in October 1979 and Baden-Wuerttemberg in March 1980. The Green party was finally in a position to make a more credible case for its ability to play a positive role in the political process through parliamentary representation—a factor considered critical for its chances in the 1980 national election where Franz Josef Strauss was the candidate for Chancellor of the CDU/CSU.

Long associated with the far right in German politics, Strauss as Chancellor was a prospect inimical to many voters who otherwise might have been sympathetic to the Greens. If the Greens were seen as having a good chance of receiving 5 percent of the vote, those supporting the environmentalists but opposed to Strauss would be less hesitant to vote Green. If, on the other hand, the Green party seemed unlikely to achieve 5 percent, voters would hesitate to vote Green because their votes would, in essence, be voided when calculating parliamentary representation, thereby enhancing the possibility of Strauss becoming Chancellor.

As it turned out, the Greens were not a significant factor in the outcome of the Bundestag elections in October 1980. In the years to follow, however, electoral results (see Table 11, Appendix) made them a force to reckon with:

- The March 1983 federal elections brought the Greens into the Bundestag, with their strong environmental platform by this time joined by an uncompromising position on nuclear disarmament—in particular their opposition to the placement of American Pershing II and cruise missiles in Europe.
- In almost every regional election since 1980, the Greens/ Alternatives received well over 5 percent of the vote.
- In Hamburg and Hesse, they denied the FDP representation in parliament.
- In two instances, Hamburg and Hesse, they held the balance of power—no majority could exist without the Greens.

For the Greens themselves, however, entering public life has had its trials and tribulations. From the party's inception, tensions have existed between those on the left who stressed economic, social, and defense-related issues and those more conservative groups who resisted dilution of the ecological principles that had initially guided the Green movement. More recently, tensions have arisen over the proper role of the Greens in the state and federal legislatures.

Having come into existence as an anti-party party, the Greens have differed over the degree to which they should engage in practices common to parliamentary politics. The "Fundos" or fundamentalists oppose collaboration and compromise, believing that such practices corrupt the principles that set the Greens apart from the established parties. The "Realos" or realists-pragmatists see cooperation and compromise as options under certain circumstances. Up to now, the willingness of the Greens to make alliances has been tested in Hamburg and Hesse.

Following the June 1982 elections in Hamburg, the Greens engaged in negotiations with the SPD over mutually acceptable terms if they were to cooperate. When they were unable to agree, a quick election in December of that same year returned an SPD majority to parliament, ending the need for an alliance. In Hesse, the September 1982 elections again left the Greens holding the balance of seats. After a delay of a year, the minority SPD government called for elections in October 1983, but the outcome still left the major parties unable to form a majority government without the Greens. After months of talks, an alliance was formed between the SPD and the Greens. The Greens voted for the state budget and confirmed the SPD prime minister in office; in return, the SPD government agreed, among other things, to a halt on the construction of new nuclear power plants. The Realos in control of the Greens in Hesse, as well, compromised on several issues, lifting their demand that all nuclear power plants in the state be closed and dropping their opposition to a new runway at the Frankfurt airport. By November 1984, however, the working coalition fell apart as the Greens announced the end of their cooperation with the SPD government after it had endorsed the expansion of nuclear fuel production facilities located in Hesse.[1]

Thus, the features unique to the German electoral system, in combination with the delicate, often precarious, representational balance among the established political parties, contrived to enhance appreciably the leverage of the environmentalists in the political process. A major consequence was that nuclear opponents were able to keep at center stage the controversies surrounding government energy policy. The situation faced the parties in the governing coalition with perplexing dilemmas:

1. At the Land level, do you—the local SPD and FDP—continue to support the energy program of the federal government, thereby increasing the prospect of defections to the Green parties, defections perhaps sufficient to keep you out of office or even out of parliament?[2] Or do you pursue a more independent line, withholding support from major elements of official energy policy, thereby making the program infinitely more difficult to execute?

2. At the national level, do you—the party leadership in government—continue to push for implementation of an energy program which, although absolutely necessary from your perspective, will accentuate divisions within the party and exacerbate relations between national leadership and Laender party organizations? Or do you back off from your announced program, thereby making the coalition government more vulnerable to attacks from the political opposition?

A PLUTONIUM ECONOMY

Electoral considerations established the tactical context of domestic politics in the Federal Republic during much of the period from 1978 on. By early 1980, with United States-Soviet relations deteriorating in the wake of the Iranian revolution and the Afghanistan occupation, the status of the Atlantic alliance and East-West détente had also become issues of concern in the campaign. During 1981–82, the issue of nuclear rearmament became more prominent as the peace movement in West Germany gained momentum, lending greater strength to the Greens. With the deepening recession during the same period, economic policy began to receive greater attention. Finally, coalition politics came to dominate certain elections; in Hesse, the FDP's tactics of abandoning the coalition in Bonn became the focal point of the election. Nevertheless, energy policy remained a principal substantive focus. The major points of controversy centered on two important components of the government's energy program: reprocessing of nuclear waste and development of the fast breeder reactor.

For several reasons, these technologies seemed crucial to the future security of German energy supply:
- By closing the nuclear fuel cycle through the reprocessing of spent fuel rods from light water reactors (LWRs), substantial amounts of unused uranium could be recovered, thereby extending the supply of uranium, which otherwise would have to be imported.

- At the same time, plutonium produced in the operation of LWRs could be extracted and later be recycled as fuel for FBRs.
- By producing more plutonium than they consumed in their operation, FBRs represented one of the few technologies which, in the longer term, promised to reduce German dependence on dwindling foreign energy supplies, whether oil, uranium, or natural gas.
- Finally, reprocessing was a necessary stage in the disposal of nuclear waste. After separating those elements that could be re-used from leftover radioactive waste products, the most radioactive and long-lasting of these wastes were to be concentrated and permanently isolated from the environment.

The waste disposal problem had become the pivotal issue relating to the further expansion of nuclear power in the Federal Republic. Central to the government's plan for nuclear waste disposal was the construction of a large, integrated facility designed to reprocess spent fuel rods and provide final burial for nuclear waste, all within a single site. This was called an *Entsorgungszentrum*. (There is no corresponding term in English. Literally translated, *Entsorgung* implies the alleviation of worry or concern.) Before 1977, this part of Germany's nuclear program received little public attention, but when further nuclear power plant construction was explicitly linked with safe disposal of nuclear waste in late 1976, pressure began to build for quicker action. The task of the private sector was to formulate plans for the reprocessing facilities; for its part, the federal government had to decide on a site suitable for long-term storage of high-level radioactive materials. Unfortunately for the government, this need for a rapid decision on the Entsorgungszentrum came just when the first effects of nationwide opposition to nuclear energy were beginning to have political impact. As a consequence, over the next several years the Entsorgung question became a political hot potato gingerly passed back and forth between federal and Laender governments.

After evaluating various methods of permanent waste disposal, federal officials had decided on burial in geologically stable salt formations, several of which were thought to be present in Lower Saxony. Accordingly, the initial step toward construction of the Entsorgungszentrum was taken by the federal government in November 1976, as it pressed the Lower Saxony government to decide on the site. However, having just witnessed the events at Wyhl and Brokdorf, Minister President Albrecht (CDU), although not wishing to scuttle the project, decided to play for time. Facing elections in spring 1978, he wanted to avoid the political problems such confrontations had created in the other CDU-governed Laender; but at the same time, since his party was a strong advocate of nuclear energy, he did not want to appear to be impeding its rapid expansion.

Albrecht's first move was to demand reconsideration of alternative methods for waste disposal, suggesting, for example, storage in the ices of Greenland, burial in the deserts of the United States, or the like. This ploy having failed, he next chose from among the disposal sites proposed by Bonn the one considered most politically unpalatable to the federal government. This was Gorleben, questionable because of its location only five kilometers from the East German border. This selection was designed both to transfer responsibility to Bonn and to create further delay in the selection of a site. But contrary to expectations, the federal government accepted the Gorleben site and by summer 1977, authorization was given to the Physikalisch-Technische Bundesanstalt, the federal agency responsible for construction of the storage facilities, to begin the studies required in the licensing process. Within the private sector, steps were also being taken. In March 1977 the DWK (*Deutsche Gesellschaft fuer Wiederaufarbeitung*), the company established by private industry to handle reprocessing, had applied to the Lower Saxony government for first stage approval of its reprocessing facilities.

As part of the studies designed to examine the suitability of the surface soil conditions and underground salt domes at the Gorleben site, test drillings were required. Anticipating a strong reaction from environmentalist groups to such an action, federal officials and Minister President Albrecht confidentially agreed that the Physikalisch-Technische Bundesanstalt would apply to the Lower Saxony government for permission to conduct test drillings only after Albrecht had given his consent—in all probability, after the elections that next spring.

This agreement was due less to the good will of the federal government, which was increasingly coming under attack from the CDU opposition for the slowdown in nuclear power plant construction, than to the particular composition of government at both federal and Laender levels. The direct negotiating partner of Albrecht in Bonn was Interior Minister Maihofer (FDP), whose party in Lower Saxony was in coalition with the CDU. Wishing to avoid difficulties for his party colleagues, Maihofer, along with his fellow FDP cabinet ministers, managed to secure the agreement. This arrangement became public after a speech given at a CDU conference in October 1977; Albrecht laid blame for delays in the nuclear program at the doorstep of the federal government, declaring that it hadn't even applied for a permit to begin the test drillings. A government spokesman subsequently released excerpts from a letter written by Albrecht to Chancellor Schmidt requesting the delay.

Delays encountered at the Land level in the licensing of the Entsorgungszentrum did not deter the federal government from moving ahead in other critical areas associated with the waste disposal problem. With the positive evaluations of the RSK and SSK for the waste disposal concept released in October 1977, the choice of a waste disposal site made, and industry's submission of an application to begin construction on the reprocessing plant, the prerequisites for renewed licensing of nuclear plant construction as defined by the federal government in March 1977 had been met. And although the original stipulations were supplemented in the revised energy program of December 1977, the added provisions were satisfied in the course of 1978. A site was chosen for an interim storage facility near Ahaus in North Rhine-Westphalia; and contracts had been concluded between the DWK and the French company Cogema for storing and reprocessing approximately 1,705 tons of spent fuel rods from German reactors between 1980 and 1984.

Several domestic critics, however, doubted whether these agreements with Cogema would really guarantee the disposal of nuclear waste for the period prescribed. They focused on two issues. First, they pointed to managerial and technical problems at the La Hague facility. Several accidents and strikes had closed the plant down for long periods, slowing plans for new expansion required to accommodate the spent fuel that had been contracted for. In addition, there were questions about the facility's ability to handle the amount of spent fuel from LWRs, which is more radioactive than the spent fuel from gas graphite reactors, the type La Hague was originally designed to handle. Second, there were objections to the provisions of the agreement. Many elements of the contract were not disclosed, leading some to suspect that there was an escape clause allowing Cogema not to accept shipments of spent fuel if, in their estimation, significant difficulties or obstacles in the construction of new interim storage tanks were encountered.[3]

Nevertheless, from the perspective of government officials, the problems of holding the spent fuel rods until the Gorleben center was ready to receive them had been resolved. Thus, all barriers to further nuclear power plant construction appeared to have been removed. Whether this view would be shared by the courts remained to be seen, especially since little progress was being made with the Entsorgungszentrum itself.

Originally, plans called for construction to begin the first part of 1979; but the June 1978 elections in Lower Saxony had come and gone and Albrecht still refused to approve applications for test drillings. Resistance to the Gorleben center had been growing, both among residents of the area, traditionally a CDU constituency, and nationwide. Because of domestic politics and political ambitions that appeared to

extend beyond the borders of Lower Saxony, Albrecht was
hesitant to take any action as the Gorleben issue had taken
on the highest priority for nuclear opponents. Only with
reprocessing could conventional nuclear power fully mature
and bring about the next step in the development of nuclear
energy, the fast breeder reactor. Strong, perhaps violent,
reactions were anticipated to any measure such as test
drillings that seemed to bring the Entsorgungszentrum
closer to reality. During this time, Albrecht entered into
negotiations with residents of the Gorleben area; and these
resulted in a decision that would further delay any action on
the center. A group of international scientists and experts
untainted by association with the nuclear industry would be
commissioned to evaluate the waste disposal concept of the
Gorleben Entsorgungszentrum.

The studies conducted in fall and winter 1978–79 culmi-
nated in a six-day hearing scheduled to begin March 28 in
Hannover. Just before the meeting, the first permits for
shallow drillings were issued. Although small demonstrations did take place near the site, they were overshadowed
by earlier preparations for a five-day march from Gorleben
to Hannover. It arrived on March 30, two days after the
hearings began and one day after the nuclear accident at
Three Mile Island. It represented the largest demonstration
ever held in West Germany to that time, with estimates of
participants exceeding 100,000.

Despite the nuclear accident at Three Mile Island, discussion at the Gorleben International Review was purposely
restricted to the issue under investigation: the safety of the
Entsorgungszentrum. The participants were divided into
two groups—the critical scientists (or *Kritiker*) and the proponents of the Gorleben project (or *Gegenkritiker*, composed
primarily of scientists and officials from the nuclear industry). Discussion centered on two points: first, whether the
experience gained from smaller, largely experimental reprocessing plants could be applied directly to the type of large-
scale reprocessing plant proposed at Gorleben; and second,
whether, in light of important problems which remained to

be solved, a decision on reprocessing should be delayed. The Kritiker proposed that numerous interim measures would allow time to study alternatives more carefully in light of current developments and more experience, thereby avoiding actions that could prove irreversible later on.

Albrecht demonstrated the importance that he attached to the questions considered in the Review by his presence and active participation in the hearings throughout the entire six days. Whether he was swayed by the arguments of the Kritiker is doubtful. Nevertheless, certain proposals made in the International Review seemed to give Albrecht an alternative to the stark choice of either beginning immediately on the reprocessing plant or scuttling the Entsorgungsgszentrum altogether. The alternative was the possibility of long-term interim storage facilities.

Approximately a month after the hearings and after over two years of delay, Albrecht announced the decision of the Lower Saxony government on the Gorleben project—an announcement carried live over German television because of public interest. While praising the Entsorgung concept of the federal government, the Minister President said, "It is possible to build such a plant without endangering the public. But, at the present time, there is such a controversy surrounding the project that it isn't feasible."[4] In other words, while he favored nuclear power in general and the Gorleben concept in particular, he opposed broad elements of the program as long as political consensus for such measures was absent.

Singled out for particular censure were those in positions of political responsibility—specifically the SPD in Lower Saxony who had demanded that the CDU government reject Gorleben despite support of the project by Chancellor Schmidt and the other federal cabinet ministers. Without agreement between a Bonn government and its sister parties in Lower Saxony, Albrecht refused permission to proceed with the reprocessing plant. He did put forward, however, certain proposals designed to salvage the nuclear program. First, the Lower Saxony government would allow shallow test drillings to continue, as well as approve deep drillings to test the suitability of the salt domes for final storage; and second, the federal government should consider the construction of long-term storage facilities for spent fuel rods as an alternative to early reprocessing.

Thus, in a dazzling display of political acumen, Albrecht had been able to block construction of the reprocessing plant in Lower Saxony and so avoid much of the anticipated conflict with anti-nuclear groups, transfer responsibility for future initiatives in the area of reprocessing and power plant construction back to Bonn, and at the same time reaffirm his basic support for nuclear energy.

This decision created certain problems for the federal government, the greatest being its potential impact on the courts. With the integrated Entsorgung concept apparently dead for the time being, officials feared that power plant construction could be delayed even longer; or worse, that the courts could demand a shutdown of plants already operating until the questions concerning waste disposal were satisfactorily resolved.

Publicly, Chancellor Schmidt directed his anger at factions in the SPD and FDP that had failed to support government energy policy; at one point, he threatened to resign. He peppered his speeches and interviews both at home and abroad with apocalyptic visions of energy shortages, increased environmental dangers such as the greenhouse effect from increased hydrocarbon consumption, and possible armed international conflict unless the nuclear option were exercised immediately.

Privately, however, he was investigating the alternatives available to the federal government in the wake of Albrecht's decision and in the face of opposition within his own party. The strategy finally adopted called for a joint federal/ Laender resolution, side-stepping for the time being any initiatives that would require immediate parliamentary approval. In late September 1979, the text of the agreement between Chancellor Schmidt and the Minister Presidents of all the Laender was announced.

Reaffirming the intention to continue working for the realization of an integrated Entsorgung concept, the resolution called for:

- The construction of interim storage facilities that could accommodate spent fuel rods for a minimum of twenty years.
- Gorleben to be the site for the final storage of nuclear waste (the government of North Rhine-Westphalia made the use of its interim storage facilities contingent upon approval of Gorleben); studies of the salt domes were to be completed as rapidly as possible in order to enable a decision to be taken during the second half of the 1980s.
- An investigation of the possibility of decentralizing reprocessing through construction of several smaller reprocessing plants.
- The consideration of final storage for spent fuel rods without reprocessing. Regardless of the technique to be used for Entsorgung—whether reprocessing or final storage without reprocessing—facilities were to be in operation by the late 1990s.

As a consequence of the joint resolution, the criteria for first stage approval had been amended somewhat:

- A preliminary choice of the site (or sites) for interim storage facilities must be made.
- The plans for these interim storage facilities must receive positive safety evaluations.
- After January 1, 1985, a preliminary choice for either a reprocessing site(s) or final storage site for unreprocessed spent fuel must be made.

Having arrived at a formula for dealing with nuclear waste, the federal government felt that the final impediments to further licensing of nuclear power plant construction had been removed.

As we saw earlier, the reprocessing issue not only had important implications for the immediate efforts of government to implement its energy program; it was also central to longer-range energy plans calling for full-scale application of the fast breeder technology by the 1990s. The government hoped to have FBRs producing up to 5 GW by the year 2000.[5] As the logical extension of current light water technology, the FBR promised economical, efficient use of a limited resource—increasing the efficiency in the use of uranium supplies by approximately sixty times. It represented one of the few possibilities of drastically reducing dependence on foreign energy sources. Nevertheless, despite this elixir-like promise, indications of growing skepticism began to appear by 1977, a skepticism that in the course of 1978–79 translated into a political force sufficient to affect government efforts to develop the fast breeder option.

First suggestions of problems to come surfaced in May 1977 as several SPD deputies in the Bundestag, threatening to break party discipline in the vote on the government's budget unless appropriations for the fast breeder program were excluded, were able to put a temporary freeze on research and development funds for fast breeder development. In August, the court case challenging the constitutionality of the FBR program was referred to the Constitutional Court. And at the November party congresses of the SPD and FDP, proposals were introduced that would require completely different licensing procedures for the FBR.

The SPD passed a resolution calling for a vote by the Bundestag before the FBR prototype at Kalkar received an operating permit and before a final decision was made on commercial development of the FBR. At the FDP congress, a motion was narrowly defeated (163 to 161) which stipulated that approval for further construction and operation of the FBR at Kalkar could only be granted after an Enquete Commission had thoroughly studied the technology and its consequences—the implication being a long delay in construction.

But it was the Greens' initial electoral successes in Hamburg and Lower Saxony that began the movement toward significant change. For the FDP, the electoral outcomes had been particularly sobering—in both Laender, they lost representation in parliament. It was not surprising, therefore, that many in the FDP made special efforts to identify the party with a deep commitment to environmental issues. Evidence of this shift was most immediately visible in North Rhine-Westphalia, where a decision on the third stage approval for Kalkar was due.

Within the SPD-FDP coalition government in North Rhine-Westphalia, several FDP members—most importantly the Economics and Interior Ministers, the key ministries in the licensing process—had become especially adamant in their opposition to the FBR. Their expressed concerns touched on the cost of the program, the possibility of accidents, and the more general problems of a plutonium economy. As an alternative, they suggested converting Kalkar from a plutonium producer (an FBR) into a facility that destroyed plutonium (a *Vernichtungsanlage*)—a proposal greeted rather coolly in Bonn.

As construction delays at Kalkar extended into fall 1978, efforts were initiated at the federal level to overcome the impasse. At the urging of Chancellor Schmidt and SPD cabinet ministers, fellow FDP cabinet members attempted to pressure their party colleagues in the North Rhine-Westphalia government to remove their veto of third stage construction at Kalkar, but to no avail. The SPD Minister President of North Rhine-Westphalia, in turn, called on the federal government to assume responsibility for a decision on further construction in the FBR project. Thus, a dynamic similar to that characterizing the reprocessing issue was now emerging in FBR development—increasing tensions between federal and Laender governments and widening divisions within the parties.

The FDP party congress held in November 1978 illustrated the growing discord. In an attempt to formulate a unified party position on the FBR, a sharp, often polemical, debate centered on two issues: first, whether to support a moratorium or renewed construction on the Kalkar project; and second, commercialization of the FBR.

The federal ministers warned against any resolution that they, as cabinet members, could not accept; representatives from North Rhine-Westphalia or the left wing of the party

remained staunchly anti-FBR. Between those factions a
rather tenuous compromise was struck, which demonstrated
the strength of opposition to the FBR. The party resolution
as finally adopted stated that the FDP rejected the commercial use of the fast breeder technology, although it didn't
directly repudiate the Kalkar project because it wasn't to be
used commercially; and the FDP demanded the creation of
an Enquete Commission to evaluate the fast breeder technology. In conjunction with this second point, third stage
approval for construction at Kalkar was to be withheld until
the findings of the Commission were presented to the Bundestag; then, on the basis of these findings, the Bundestag
was to make a decision.

Thus, the FDP called for measures that would result in
considerable delay while the Commission made its report
and would transfer responsibility for licensing of the FBR
from the Land to the federal level.

On the face of it, this relatively strong anti-FBR position
offered little hope for finding a quick solution to the stalemate in North Rhine-Westphalia. It did, however, suggest
potential areas of accommodation. Negotiations between
SPD and FDP leaders were initiated at the federal level; and
by mid-December, an agreement had been worked out and
adopted by the Bundestag. It called for a parliamentary vote
on the resolution approving renewed construction at Kalkar
and the creation of a commission composed of Bundestag
deputies and scientists to study the FBR.

Emphasizing the importance attached to the resolution by
the leadership of both parties—as well as their concerns
about its passage—it was tied to a vote of confidence. In spite
of this added pressure to maintain party discipline, six FDP
deputies abstained, pointing out that they rather than the
party leaders were the ones adhering to party policy as
formulated by the full membership the previous month at
the party congress. That policy called for no decision to be
made until the study on uses and risks of the FBR had been
completed.

Despite this incident, the vote seemed to clear the way for

third stage approval of the Kalkar project. With the burden of responsibility shifted to the Bundestag, the Economics Minister for North Rhine-Westphalia declared, "We will not delay. There will be no artificial difficulties."[6]

The fragile consensus on nuclear power represented in the revised energy program of December 1977 was thus shattered by the forces of electoral politics. With the Green parties often able to dictate the content of political debate— the desirability of nuclear power in general, of reprocessing and FBR development in particular—divisions within the established political parties were exacerbated and tensions between Laender and federal governments surfaced. Under pressure from the grass roots, regional party organizations were increasingly coming into conflict with their national party leaders over energy policy, and Laender governments were continually thwarting the implementation of the government's energy program. Nevertheless, the controversy within the Federal Republic over reprocessing and FBR development was not attributable solely to the workings of domestic politics.

NUCLEAR POWER AND NON-PROLIFERATION

In the early 1970s, United States government officials undertook a fundamental reevaluation of the nation's approach to nuclear non- proliferation. With the explosion of a nuclear device by India in May 1974 serving as catalyst, the U.S. government initiated efforts to revise the international rules and norms that had governed non-proliferation since the 1960s and that had been institutionalized in the International Atomic Energy Agency (IAEA). Believing that detection alone of unauthorized diversions of nuclear fuel from civil power programs by an IAEA inspection system was no longer sufficient to prevent the spread of nuclear weapons, the United States called for "full-scope" safeguards as well as a ban on the future export of reprocessing technologies. Contrasted with earlier arrangements, full-scope safeguards required the submission of *all* a state's peaceful nuclear

activities, whether imported or indigenous, to IAEA safeguarding and inspection in recipient countries, regardless of
whether they had signed the Non-Proliferation Treaty
(NPT).

At the international level, U.S. efforts toward more effective prevention of proliferation first bore fruit with an interim agreement among nuclear supplier states on procedures for safeguarding certain nuclear exports. Original
members of what came to be known as the London suppliers
group were the United States, the U.S.S.R., the United
Kingdom, West Germany, Japan, France, and Canada, with
Belgium, the Netherlands, Italy, Sweden, Switzerland,
Czechoslovakia, East Germany, and Poland joining later.

In August 1974, a "trigger list" of materials and facilities
was drawn up by supplier countries and submitted to the
IAEA. This interim agreement was followed the next year,
1975, by the formulation of a set of guidelines stipulating
that "government assurance" should be given "explicitly
excluding uses which would result in any nuclear explosive."
In addition, suppliers promised to use "restraint in the
transfer of sensitive facilities, technology, and weapons-
usable materials" and "prudence" to avoid the production of
any nuclear material not safeguarded.[7] In essence, the
states agreed not to export specified materials to non-nuclear weapon states without prior agreement with the IAEA
on the application of safeguards, assurances against their
use for any nuclear explosive device, and the prohibition of
re-export to non-nuclear weapon states not party to the NPT
without IAEA safeguards.[8] And although U.S. proposals for
full-scope safeguards and a ban on the export of reprocessing
technology were not included, these agreements among the
supplier states did represent significant movement within
the international community toward the new American position on non-proliferation. In order to re-enforce its commitment to non-proliferation, however, the United States
also initiated unilateral measures designed to discourage
the spread of nuclear weapons.

In October 1976, the Ford administration announced a

moratorium on the commercial reprocessing of spent fuel "unless there is a sound reason to determine that the world community can effectively overcome the risks of proliferation."[9] That next year, under a new administration, a statement was issued on U.S. nuclear policy which contained the following points:

1. Commercial reprocessing and plutonium recycle were to be delayed indefinitely.
2. The U.S. breeder reactor program was to be restructured, and the date for breeder commercialization deferred.
3. A U.S. inquiry into less proliferative alternate fuel cycles was to be undertaken.
4. U.S. productive capacity for low enrichment fuel was to be increased.
5. Legislation was to be introduced to permit the offering of nuclear fuel supply contracts and guaranteed delivery.
6. Embargos on exports of enrichment or reprocessing technology were to continue.
7. Among other negotiations, the establishment of an international fuel cycle evaluation program aimed at exploring technologies and arrangements to reduce the risk of proliferation was to be sought.[10]

And finally, in conjunction with point five, the Nuclear Non-Proliferation Act (NNPA) was signed into law by President Carter on April 7, 1978. Among other things, NNPA contained:

provisions for immediate cessation of U.S. exports to any non-nuclear-weapon state that terminates, abrogates, or materially violates IAEA safeguards, or that engages in any activity of direct significance to the acquisition of nuclear explosive devices. Exports to any state may be terminated if it violates agreements on nuclear technology transfer, assists a non-nuclear-weapon state with activities pursuant to the acquisition of a nuclear explosive, or enters into an agreement for the transfer of reprocessing except in connection with an international arrangement to which the U.S. subscribes (unless the President determines that such action would run counter to U.S. non-proliferation policies). Export licensing criteria include provisions for application of IAEA safeguards, no use of exports for explosive-related purposes, provision of adequate physical security based on U.S. guidelines, U.S. consent for retransfers or reprocessing of U.S. supplied material or equipment produced through any transferred sensitive nuclear technology.[11]

In the wake of this changing American perception on non-proliferation and subsequent measures initiated by the United States to encourage other countries to adopt a similar orientation, the German government's nuclear program, already under fire from internal critics, had become the focus of increasing external pressures. The already intricate web of domestic actors and objectives confronting policymakers was made even more complex with the intrusion of foreign actors attempting to influence the content and direction of German energy policy.

While non-proliferation was not an issue of serious debate in the controversy over nuclear power within the Federal Republic, at least three elements central to German nuclear policy were challenged directly or indirectly by the new initiatives of the United States: a commercially strong and viable national nuclear industry, reprocessing, and FBR development.

We have already discussed how government and industrial interests in the Federal Republic collaborated closely to develop a German nuclear industry that not only would supply domestic demand but also provide a product competitive in the international market. (By 1977, public expenditures on nuclear technology had amounted to over DM 17.5 billion.) These efforts seemed to be vindicated in 1975, when the largest sale in the history of the nuclear industry was concluded between the Federal Republic and Brazil. It was the first time a non-American company had successfully broken into a world market that, up to that time, had been monopolized by Westinghouse and General Electric.[12] However, the key determinant in KWU's winning out over Westinghouse—its ability to include reprocessing and enrichment facilities in the commercial package—was precisely what set the German government's intention to promote its nuclear export sector at loggerheads with an American government's increasing concern about the implications of these technologies for nuclear proliferation.

Informed by the German government of the impending agreement with Brazil, the U.S. government voiced its opposition. Many West Germans, on the other hand, felt that American protestations were based primarily on commercial self-interest rather than on non-proliferation concerns. Such suspicions were rooted in earlier experiences: American industry and government officials had purportedly snatched orders from KWU by promises of "unfair" interest rates from the Import-Export Bank (in the case of Yugoslavia), warnings that no enriched uranium would be available from the United States if American reactors were not purchased (in the cases of Yugoslavia and Spain), and threats of withholding economic assistance if a German reactor were bought (in the case of Argentina).[13]

When subsequent contacts with German officials convinced the Ford administration that the Germans were intent on concluding the deal, however, an American negotiating team was dispatched to Bonn to suggest certain changes in the agreement. These suggestions were based on earlier U.S. experience with non-NPT countries, as well as on the lessons provided by India.[14] And although the extent of U.S. influence is difficult to determine, the tripartite agreement between the Federal Republic, Brazil, and the IAEA was the strictest ever concluded with a non-NPT state.[15]

Nevertheless, press criticism was scathing. In an edito-

rial, the *New York Times* referred to the actions of West
Germany and Brazil as "nuclear madness" and described
the deal as a "reckless move that could set off a nuclear arms
race in Latin America, trigger the nuclear arming of a
half-dozen nations elsewhere, and endanger the United
States and the world as a whole."[16] Congressional reaction
was equally severe: "Congressmen active in nuclear matters
were not content with improvements, and Senator Pastore,
chairman of the Joint Committee on Atomic Energy, was
particularly convinced that the transaction was irremedia-
bly detrimental to American and world interests and that it
had to be stopped. Congress's implacable position was that
Kissinger and Ford must not shrink from a high-level
confrontation, and that the United States should even reconsider its NATO commitment to Germany if this were
necessary to demonstrate American seriousness."[17] Further,
treatment of the non-proliferation issue during the 1976
presidential race foreshadowed a renewed American effort
to have the Brazilian deal canceled.

   During the campaign and before the inauguration, Carter
had singled out the German-Brazilian deal for special criticism. As evidence of the concern raised by these attacks in
Bonn, Undersecretary of State Peter Hermes was dispatched
to Washington even before the inauguration in an effort to
forestall any further public pronouncements that would
commit the incoming administration to a position opposing
the Brazilian deal.[18] Once in office, the Carter administration immediately began to exert pressures on the German
government to reconsider the export of reprocessing and
enrichment facilities. During the first official visit of a
high-ranking member of the Carter administration, Vice
President Mondale urgently requested that the Germans
forego delivery of the sensitive technologies. This was then
followed up by two rounds of negotiations conducted by
Deputy Secretary of State Warren Christopher.[19] Nevertheless, the German government remained, and has remained,
adamant. Its position is perhaps attributable to two factors.
The first is fundamental differences between the two gov-

ernments over the appropriate approach to non-proliferation.

Although both the United States and the Federal Republic profess strong support for the goal of nuclear non-proliferation, considerable disagreement exists about the means
of achieving this goal. For the United States, denial of
"sensitive technologies," such as reprocessing and enrichment facilities, to countries not already possessing them is
considered the most effective approach. The German government, on the other hand, believes that it is critical to
include states in agreements that provide adequate safeguards against abuses of these technologies. Bonn considers
it better to make available the complete fuel cycle to countries that legitimately seek greater independence in energy
supply under strictly controlled conditions than to force
these countries to develop such capabilities on their own,
outside of effective external controls. Skeptics, however,
might see this egalitarian view as serving very well the
commercial interests of the German nuclear industry. The
ability to offer the complete nuclear fuel cycle gives KWU a
considerable competitive edge over the American giants in
the international market, since Westinghouse and GE are
forbidden by the American government to export such sensitive technologies.

The second consideration behind German intransigence is
the commercial importance that the Brazilian sales came to
assume for domestic industry. Because of the de facto moratorium on nuclear power plant construction in West Germany, the domestic market for nuclear reactors had atro-
phied rapidly. KWU had not received a single domestic order
between 1975 and 1979, a serious matter for an industry half
of whose yearly production capacity (four of eight reactors)
was allocated for the internal market. With declining domestic sales, the foreign market took on an even greater
importance. Without the foreign orders received by KWU in
1975 from Brazil and in 1976 for two reactors from Iran, the
German nuclear industry would have been in great danger
of folding.

Thus, the pressures from the United States to cancel the Brazilian deal and to renounce further sales of sensitive technologies threatened to limit the competitiveness of German nuclear exports internationally and in the process to endanger the viability of an important industrial sector. The German government had hoped for rapid expansion in the nuclear export market to strengthen the country's extremely important foreign trade position. We have seen that government officials viewed the country's ability to compete in the international market place as closely linked to the success of high technology products such as nuclear reactors. Both the BMFT and BMWi were strong supporters of KWU's push into the international market. U.S. non-proliferation policy not only focused on the *transfer* of certain "proliferating" technologies, however; it directed attention to their *domestic use* as well.

In April 1977, President Carter announced an indefinite delay in U.S. commercial reprocessing and the long-term storage of spent fuel elements. Although the President explicitly said, "We are not trying to impose our will on those nations like Japan, France, Britain, and Germany which already have reprocessing plants in operation," his announcement contained a proposal for discussion of the nuclear fuel cycle within an international framework—a clear "invitation" for other countries to consider similar measures.[20]

In October 1977, an International Nuclear Fuel Cycle Evaluation (INFCE) commenced its consideration of questions relating to the nuclear fuel cycle. Eight working groups were established to cover fuel and heavy water, enrichment, long-term supply, reprocessing, fast breeders, spent fuel, waste management and disposal, advanced fuel cycle, and reactor concepts. For the Federal Republic, such an initiative could hardly have come at a worse time. The question of further power plant construction was being linked to the resolution of the waste disposal problem; and the controversy over the concept of the central integrated Entsorgungszentrum was beginning to heat up. The new U.S. policy highlighted the fundamental differences be-

tween the two countries over reprocessing, and the conflict was exploited by the domestic opponents of nuclear
power.

The decision by the Carter administration to delay commercial reprocessing was viewed somewhat skeptically by
officials in Bonn. For one, they pointed out that reprocessing
had only been delayed in the commercial arena—for military purposes, development of reprocessing technology continued. In addition, Bonn called attention to the presence of
vast energy resources in the United States—oil, natural gas,
uranium, coal—which allowed the American government to
delay a decision on reprocessing. The Federal Republic,
lacking such abundant energy supplies, had to make the
most efficient use of its fuel. And finally, the Bonn government pointed out that, until very recently, both countries
had favored reprocessing because of its ecological as well as
its economic benefits; to separate highly radioactive waste
through reprocessing and to store it in solidified form was
environmentally much safer than the long-term storage of
spent fuel rods.[21]

These differences, among others, were to constitute the
substance of negotiations conducted within INFCE; and
although German participation in the conference was never
really in doubt, it was guaranteed with assurances from U.S.
officials that all decisions relating to the issues under discussion at INFCE would be held in abeyance until the
Evaluation had been concluded, a period of approximately
two years. With the passage of the aforementioned Nuclear
Non-Proliferation Act of 1978, however, the German nuclear
program again became a target of U.S. non-proliferation
policy.

Unilaterally establishing conditions for the export of nuclear material, this new law severely circumscribed the use
of uranium enriched in the United States while requiring all
agreements previously concluded with the United States to
be renegotiated. If countries were found in violation of the
NNPA or refused to renegotiate, U.S. exports of nuclear
materials were to cease immediately. Because the Federal
Republic received 60 to 65 percent of all enriched uranium

used commercially from the United States and 100 percent of the uranium used in its research reactors, the implications of this legislation were immense. German decisions on such politically sensitive questions as reprocessing, retransfer and storage of plutonium or spent fuel rods, and the export of nuclear material to third states would be subject to American approval.

Understandably, the American action did little to enhance relations between the U.S. and German governments, especially after the reassurances received by the Germans earlier on this issue. The Federal Republic, along with certain other Western European countries, primarily France, balked at renegotiating a contract that specified U.S. delivery of enriched uranium up to 1995. But owing to a special provision in the NNPA, more serious confrontation was averted. The law provided a two-year grace period for details of a renegotiated agreement to be worked out if Euratom—the official broker between members of the European Community and outside suppliers of nuclear fuel—affirmed its willingness to enter into negotiations within thirty days. And although this deadline lapsed without agreement, a modus operandi was finally established that postponed, at least until March 1980, any firm actions stemming from the NNPA. American and German officials agreed that the European Community would enter into "talks" with the United States which would be more or less non-binding, not making an issue over the subtle difference between "talks" and "negotiations."[22] In the meantime, the more controversial questions touching on reprocessing, waste disposal, and plutonium technologies were to be discussed within the framework of INFCE.

Central to the Carter administration's strategy of nonproliferation, and closely related to its policy on reprocessing, was the deferring of a decision on commercialization of the fast breeder reactor. When weighed against the problems associated with early commercial use of the FBR, the gains—whether of enhanced energy supply or economic benefits—were seen as minimal at best. The Americans saw anticipation of early FBR commercialization as a major motive behind the push for facilities to reprocess spent fuel from LWRs. But possession of reprocessing facilities, it was felt, would make possible the quicker acquisition of nuclear weapons. Further, because the amount of plutonium produced and in circulation would grow appreciably with the widespread application of FBR technology, it could become a target of theft for terrorist groups. The FBR technology raised issues of health and safety as well.[23]

These reservations were not shared by several European countries, West Germany included. Once it became clear that Carter's FBR policy was to apply beyond U.S. boundaries, with FBR technology a major topic at INFCE, the issue became another bone of contention between the American and German governments. As in the case of reprocessing, the American initiatives concerning FBRs came at a very inopportune time; domestic opposition was increasing substantially throughout this 1977–78 period.

In response to the newly defined policy of the Carter administration, as well as to the growing number of domestic critics, a report was published by the BMFT that detailed the government's position on FBR development. The report held, in regard to health and safety, that FBRs represented no qualitatively greater risks than the LWRs or certain other industrial activities using highly toxic substances.[24] Regarding theft, the plutonium from FBRs was a relatively ineffective material for use by terrorist groups. There were several toxic materials more easily acquired and faster acting; in addition, natural, technical, and organizational barriers militated against the theft and effective utilization of plutonium in nuclear bombs.[25]

The report pointed out that the large domestic energy resources of the United States put it in a much better position to postpone the commercial phase of FBR development than was the Federal Republic. German officials were, in fact, quite skeptical about whether Carter's FBR policy actually would result in deferment of commercial use. They pointed out that FBR development continued in the United

States, to the tune of $450 million in 1978, more than the entire 1978 BMFT budget for nuclear energy; Moreover, the President's initiative was still being disputed in Congress.[26] Whatever the Americans thought or did, however, the West Germans believed early commercialization of the FBR to be crucial, not only for economic but strategic reasons as well.

Aside from reducing Germany's dependence on oil, one strategic consideration—although not often articulated publicly—was lessening dependence on foreign uranium supplies. In 1974, the United States had defaulted on long-term supply contracts with Euratom and in 1975 delivery of nuclear materials was temporarily halted; in 1977, Canada had abruptly imposed an embargo on the export of uranium to the European Community; and the NNPA of 1978 threatened an American embargo on uranium supplies. FBR development was seen as a way to reduce the Federal Republic's vulnerability to such embargoes.

Finally, the BMFT report disputed the American belief that commercialization of the FBR would increase the possibility of nuclear proliferation. The report argued, first, that although plutonium was produced in greater amounts by the FBR than by other nuclear activities, the problem of non-proliferation was not specific to the breeder technology. Second, if a country intended to acquire a nuclear capability, there were much simpler and faster ways of going about it. And finally, proliferation was a problem requiring a political solution during the next decade, a period in which the FBR would be of little commercial significance.[27]

This government report provided documentation of the broad and fundamental differences over FBR development that marked the American and German positions. However, in contrast to the contentious atmosphere that sometimes clouded U.S.-German relations because of conflicting nuclear export and reprocessing policies, the differences over fast breeder technology remained muted and discussion of these divergent positions took place primarily within the multilateral framework of INFCE.

As key elements of German nuclear policy were brought into question by U.S. efforts to redefine the rules governing non-proliferation, we need to examine the effect of these initiatives on the nuclear program of the Schmidt government.

In the case of FBR development, the effect has perhaps been more inferential than tangible. The BMFT government report, primarily a response to the critique of the German fast breeder program implicit in the Carter position, reflected considerable concern about the impact of American policy on the debate in West Germany. Historically, developments in the U.S. nuclear sector have had significant impact on nuclear policy choices in Western Europe; the commercial dominance of the LWR is one example. Official U.S. opposition to early FBR commercialization threatened to enhance the credibility of domestic critics, strengthening the ability of FBR opponents in West Germany to affect the outcome of the internal debate. Indeed, Carter's statement in April 1977 reportedly had been a factor that contributed to growing reservations about the German FBR program when opposition within the coalition parties was starting to coalesce.[28]

The effect of U.S. non-proliferation policy on reprocessing was considerable. As in the FBR controversy, Carter's decision to delay reprocessing seemed to lend greater respectability to domestic critics. Whereas reprocessing had originally been considered indispensable to the nuclear program, the U.S. example provided opponents with proposals for what could be regarded as realistic, viable alternatives to immediate reprocessing. Proposals such as final storage of spent fuel without reprocessing have subsequently been given more careful consideration by government officials, and, in the instance of long-term interim storage, such a proposal is being implemented. In addition, the U.S. Nuclear Non-proliferation Act, in the light of past German dependence on American enriched uranium, has given the United States great potential leverage over certain policy areas, such as reprocessing, export of nuclear fuel to third countries, and the like.

Finally, the impact of American non-proliferation efforts on German nuclear export policy has been somewhat mixed. On the one hand, while the Federal Republic has refused to cancel the Brazilian deal despite intense U.S. pressures, it did give a commitment to discontinue the export of reprocessing technology "until further notice." On the other hand, the West German government has more recently endorsed the sale of a heavy water reactor to Argentina without requiring full-scope safeguards.

As originally conceived, the heavy water reactor was to be part of a package which included a large heavy water production plant. With a Canadian company also bidding for the project, the German government supposedly reached an understanding with the Canadians that full-scope safeguards would be required. The Argentinian government, however, split the package, giving the reactor contract to KWU and the plant contract to a Swiss firm. And since the Swiss weren't demanding a full-scope commitment, the Germans maintained that they shouldn't be expected to demand more, especially since the plant was the much more sensitive (proliferative) technology. Some type of collusion was suspected by the Canadians: the German reactor bid was $1.6 billion, compared to $1.1 billion by the Canadians. Argentine officials, however, said they gave the contract to the Germans because of their better performance record in Argentina.

It appears that the U.S. non-proliferation policy has had an effect on German nuclear policy, but the full impact is at present difficult to assess because the domestic debate and international dialogue have fused, leaving unresolved the major questions involving the future of nuclear power.

AN END TO THE NUCLEAR STALEMATE?

Moving into the 1980s, the future of nuclear power in West Germany remains ambiguous. On the one hand, the cumulative effect of several recent developments has led to guarded optimism regarding the nuclear sector.

The administrative courts have lifted the construction stops imposed earlier at Grohnde, Brokdorf, and Wyhl. Work was resumed at Grohnde in 1978 and Brokdorf in 1981, although at Wyhl a new application for the initial construction permit (1. TEG) has been required because of changes in the building plans.

With oil prices skyrocketing in the wake of the second oil crisis and instability continuing in the Gulf region, the government's justification of nuclear power, as reflected in the Third Revision of the Energy Program of November 1981, was much less equivocal. Where the Second Revision called for only a limited expansion of nuclear energy, the Third Revision urged an increasing role for nuclear power in the electricity-generating sector, though the government again refused to offer an official target.

Acting on this renewed commitment, the federal government, in consultation with the Laender, approved a catalogue of measures designed to streamline the licensing process. One of the central simplifications was the standardization of nuclear plant designs. Within months—in February 1982—for the first time in over four years and after a delay of five years, construction on three new nuclear power plants was authorized by the Interior Ministry in "convoy." That is, with the three plants following a standard design, licensing was to proceed more or less simultaneously in all Laender, with clearance in one state making clearance in the others automatic.

The three construction permits were granted on the basis of an assessment by the government that the criteria for waste disposal were being satisfied. More specifically, on-site storage capacity was increasing through the use of compact storage of spent fuel rods (*Kompaktlager*); two interim storage sites, at Gorleben and Ahaus in North Rhine-Westphalia, had been chosen, with construction beginning on both during 1983. In that same year, applications for permits had been filed for two reprocessing plants, one at

Dragehn in Lower Saxony and the other at Wackersdorf in Bavaria; the government gave preliminary approval for the Bavarian site in 1985. Finally, although contracted shipments of spent fuel rods to France for reprocessing were temporarily halted while a debate on the future direction of French nuclear policy was conducted following the 1981 election victory of the Socialists, deliveries subsequently were resumed.

After detailed study by the Second Bundestag Enquete Commission and extended negotiations between the federal government, electrical utilities, and industrial firms in the nuclear field, the new CDU/CSU-FDP government decided in April 1983 to complete the fast breeder at Kalkar. The negotiations dealt with the amount of additional money the private sector was willing to commit to the project. The funds finally agreed on for completion were: federal government, DM 697.5 million; utilities, DM 170 million; industrial firms, DM 180 million. When construction began ten years earlier, the estimated cost was less than DM 1 billion; by 1983, the figure had risen to DM 6.5 billion. The Enquete Commission had recommended that the Bundestag lift its reservations on the completion of the Kalkar reactor but it also said that the reactor should be commissioned only after explicit political approval of the Bundestag.

Finally, the international pressures to delay domestic development of the FBR and reprocessing because of concern about nuclear proliferation had abated considerably by the early 1980s. The International Nuclear Fuel Cycle Evaluation (INFCE), with certain qualifications, found that these technologies could play an appropriate role in the nuclear programs of countries like West Germany. On balance, the findings at INFCE appeared weighted in favor of the Europeans. Although acknowledging that reprocessing posed proliferation risks, they did not conclude that reprocessing should be foregone. In addition, INFCE found that FBRs could provide significant economic advantages to countries such as West Germany without any greater risk of proliferation than existed from the current reactors.[29] In addition, non-proliferation was given a lower priority by the incoming Reagan administration, which, in any case, supported the FBR program and resumption of civilian reprocessing and did not oppose similar policies in "reliable" countries overseas.

Despite these positive signs, however, economic, political and juridical uncertainties persist, dampening optimism about nuclear power in the Federal Republic.

Doubts remain regarding the viability of the government's revised formula for nuclear waste disposal. An administrative court ruled in September 1981 that the strategy of increasing on-site storage capacity by the use of Kompaktlager, with its closer placement of spent fuel rods, violated the Atom Law. Although an upper court registered doubt about the permissibility of compact storage under the law, it allowed the practice to continue for the time being. Regarding the shipments of spent fuel rods to France for reprocessing, many are still concerned that confidential clauses in the contracts may allow the company to refuse to accept and reprocess German spent fuel at any time in the future. Finally, initial results from the studies done on the Gorleben salt domes to be used for final storage have reportedly offered little reason for optimism.[30]

Public opposition to nuclear power appears to remain strong. A survey conducted by Allensbach Institute in October 1981 found that 57 percent of those polled opposed nuclear energy, a slight increase over previous polls. In the areas of Hesse under consideration as sites for a reprocessing plant, strong anti-nuclear sentiment probably persuaded the federal government to drop Hesse from consideration. In the communal elections of Volksmarsen held in March 1981, a group whose only electoral platform consisted of opposition to a proposed reprocessing facility received 42 percent of the vote.

Party politics continues to feel the effect of the anti-nuclear sentiment. While it was still in government, the SPD suffered a widening gap between the national leadership and local membership. In the months preceding the

SPD Berlin party congress in December 1979, several party organizations had expressed opposition to nuclear power in regions such as Schleswig-Holstein, Hamburg, Lower Saxony, Hesse, and Baden-Wuerttemberg. The Third Revision—unequivocal in its support for nuclear energy—appeared to discard much of the party's policy on nuclear power that had been articulated at the Berlin Congress. With Chancellor Schmidt using all the influence at his disposal in an election year, a compromise was struck at the congress reservedly in favor of a limited expansion of nuclear energy, but only to close possible gaps in energy supply unable to be filled by coal. A large share of the party, nevertheless, supported a much more anti-nuclear stance. The Revision also downplayed the conclusions of the first Enquete Commission created by the Bundestag to study future nuclear energy policy. This commission, appointed by the Bundestag and composed of parliamentary deputies and scientists, concluded a year-long study in June 1980, recommending postponement of any further nuclear power development for ten years. Chancellor Schmidt's support of the CDU government in Schleswig-Holstein on construction of the Brokdorf reactor in the face of regional SPD opposition contributed to the resignation of Hamburg's Social Democratic mayor and leader of the SPD in Schleswig-Holstein. Following approval of the 2. TEG by Schleswig-Holstein, the Hamburg SPD voted to withdraw the city-owned utility from its 50 percent participation in the Brokdorf project. Federal officials, in response, made it clear that Veba would be asked to step in if Hamburg pulled out. The FDP, locked in a struggle for survival, is loath to advocate policies that would push additional voters toward the Greens. For example, going into March 1984 regional elections in Baden-Wuerttemberg, the FDP made it clear that a "no" to construction of the Wyhl nuclear power plant was required if a coalition government was to be formed with the CDU. And even with the CDU/CSU now leading the government, there is little sign of new initiatives that would change the prospects for nuclear power. In fact, a familiar pattern, like that followed by the SPD when it was in government, began to reappear. In fall 1983, leading up to regional elections in Baden-Wuerttemberg the next year, the CDU Minister President postponed indefinitely construction of a nuclear power plant near the Wyhl site that was scheduled to begin in 1984. He feared that the SPD would make nuclear power the major issue of the election.

Finally, and perhaps most tellingly, the private sector has yet to manifest any great degree of confidence in the long-run viability of nuclear power. Evaluations of recent economic trends have been pessimistic, or at least uncertain. For example, demand for electricity has increased at a slower rate recently and lower growth for electrical consumption is projected into the 1990s.[31] There is great uncertainty about the effects of economic slowdown and recovery on these figures; but even if demand continues to grow, there are questions about how price competitive nuclear power will be against oil and natural gas in view of recent trends in the world oil market and the direction of energy prices. Taken together, the political obstacles and practical questions raised by nuclear power have resulted in there being only one order for a nuclear plant since 1975, with no further orders on the horizon.

Thus, despite the continued support of successive governments from both the center-left and center-right, the future for nuclear power in the Federal Republic of Germany is far from assured. The reasons have very much to do with the structural features of the German political system itself. It is a type of federalism in which substantial power and authority reside at the Land level, with noticeable effects on the licensing process for nuclear facilities. The provisions in the system for judicial review have been used by nuclear opponents with notable success. And the electoral and parliamentary system has enhanced the influence of the Greens both directly, in their ability to affect electoral outcomes and the formation of governing coalitions, and indirectly in their impact on intra-party policy debates and positions by their appeal to certain constituencies in the traditional political parties. When combined, these features offer a wealth of access points to groups who wish to engage in the political process.

6. Nuclear Power and the French State

As we saw earlier, in both France and West Germany comprehensive energy strategies were articulated in response to dramatic shifts in the world energy market. The countries were both strongly committed to nuclear power as the prime means of reducing their dependence on increasingly expensive, insecure supplies of imported oil. Nevertheless, there has been a vast disparity in their ability to translate this common commitment into action. In sharp contrast to the Federal Republic, where efforts to implement its nuclear program were continually frustrated by vigorous anti-nuclear forces within the country, the French state, despite comparable levels of domestic opposition throughout much of the 1970s, has been undeterred in its policy of rapid nuclear expansion. We will see why in this chapter.

Relative differences in natural resources may partially explain the divergent outcomes. With little in the way of indigenous energy resources, the French government has few other policy options if it wishes to become less dependent on oil imports. Yet, however important such variances in domestic energy sources may be for a country's energy policy, this alone does not explain the difference between West Germany and France.

In the previous chapter, we saw how the German situation demonstrated the importance of political and social as well as economic factors in shaping the content and direction of energy policy. In the analysis to follow we will see that the institutions and traditions of the French polity, too, have left their indelible mark on France's nuclear program. With this in mind, let us look, first, at the actual policies undertaken by French energy officials in the nuclear sector; second, at the domestic and foreign challenges to those policies; and third, at certain features of the political system that have served to insulate the French state from the pressures of the anti-nuclear forces.

THE FRENCH NUCLEAR PROGRAM

As the effects of the oil embargo and four-fold price hikes of 1973–74 reverberated through the economies of the industrialized West, French officials proposed one of the most ambitious nuclear programs in the world. The extent of their commitment to nuclear power is reflected in the figures contained in the program as it evolved through the 1970s:

- In the midst of the energy crisis, March 1974, the government called for a speedup of the nuclear program, with construction to increase from 2000 MW in 1973 to 6000 MW in 1974, 6000MW in 1975, and 6–7000 MW per year through 1980. The foundation for this rapid expansion was laid in 1971 with the government decision to construct ten LWRs over the next five years.[1]
- In 1975, this decision was formalized in a comprehensive program calling for nuclear energy to meet 25 percent of France's total energy needs by 1985—up from only 2 percent in 1973. Accordingly, Electricité de France (EDF) was authorized in February 1975 to build 12,000 MW during 1976–77—approximately six plants per year.
- In 1976, it was decided to limit construction over the next two years (1977–78) to 5000 MW per year for reasons largely to do with slower growth in the demand for electricity.
- In April 1979, however, in the wake of the second oil crisis, the government announced a renewed acceleration of nuclear power construction—an added 5000 MW output

every year—followed in 1980 by a revision of the government's long-term energy program, reaffirming the role nuclear power was to play over the next decade. By 1990, nuclear was to provide 30 percent of primary energy consumption, up from the 1978 level of 3.5 percent.

- Finally, and over the longer term, the fast breeder reactor was to assume an ever more important role in nuclear power generation; from 1985 to the year 2000, two FBRs were expected to be ordered every three years.[2]

While construction on nuclear facilities in most other major industrialized countries of the West slackened through the second half of the 1970s and the long-term viability of nuclear power remained cloudy, the French government's commitment to nuclear power has never relented. In committing itself to the rapid expansion of nuclear power, however, the government had no desire simply to replace dependence on imported oil with dependence on foreign nuclear technology and material. Consequently, a wholesale restructuring of the nuclear industry was undertaken as well, a process having its roots in earlier technological choices.

In 1945 the provisional government had created the Commissariat à l'Energie Atomique (CEA), a public body charged with the responsibility of developing nuclear energy.[3] Dictated largely by military considerations, the nuclear technology chosen for development was the gas-graphite reactor. For several reasons, this was preferable to other technologies. It used natural uranium, thereby freeing France from any dependence on the United States for enriched uranium; and plutonium was produced more easily in this type of reactor, thus providing fissionable materials which could be used for nuclear weapons. These military considerations became less critical, however, by the early 1960s, when France's *force de frappe* had become a reality. In addition, the French nuclear arsenal was shifting from atomic to hydrogen bombs, thereby reducing plutonium requirements. Pressures then began to build within France for a reorientation of French nuclear and industrial policy.

By the mid-1960s, EDF was becoming increasingly skeptical about the prospects of a gas-graphite reactor that could compare favorably with the LWR in cost and efficiency. In 1964, the British government had abandoned the development of its natural uranium technology; and in that same year, the first commercial sale of a LWR had been made in the United States. The CEA, on the other hand, continued to push for the development and commercialization of the technology that it had nurtured from inception. The ensuing struggle over the future control of nuclear power in France left the nuclear sector in a state of paralysis. Serious technical problems encountered in EDF's largest experimental gas-graphite reactor almost immediately after its start-up in fall 1966 resulted in recriminations from both sides. In winter 1967–68, EDF rejected bids for the construction of two gas-graphite reactors because of unacceptably high costs. Toward the end of the decade, support from French industrial groups, along with the influential PEON commission (*Commission Consultative pour la production d'electricité d'origine nucléaire*) swung to the light water technology.

Initially, French industrial interests were favorably disposed to the gas-graphite technology, because its commercial use held the promise of a protected market; however, with no domestic orders forthcoming and little prospect of sales overseas, support shifted to the LWR—the technology expected to dominate the international market. With the expansion of Westinghouse and its light water technology into several European countries by 1968, the arguments that the French nuclear industry had to reorganize to compete in the world market increasingly impressed government officials.

Reflecting this growing support for the LWR, including a number of proponents emerging within the CEA itself, the PEON commission—composed primarily of the highest-ranking officials in EDF, CEA, the nuclear industry, the Plan, and the Ministries of Finance and Industry—recommended the construction of several LWRs, basing their judgment on assessments of electricity produced 15 percent cheaper than in gas-graphite reactors.[4]

In November 1969, shortly after the resignation of de Gaulle, newly-elected President Georges Pompidou decided to abandon the gas-graphite reactor in favor of the American LW technology. Following this abandonment, the market for LWRs was shared between CGE, a company under license to General Electric, and Framatome, the French licensee of Westinghouse. Westinghouse owned 45 percent of Framatome; the French industrial group Creusot-Loire held a 51 percent share. In 1975, as the nuclear program began to accelerate, the government granted Framatome a monopoly for the construction of LWRs in France. At the same time, it initiated efforts to reduce the role of the American company in the French nuclear sector: in 1976 an agreement was worked out with Westinghouse that transferred 30 percent of its holdings in Framatome to the CEA, the final 15 percent to follow in 1982 when the license ran out. The purpose was Frenchification of the light water technology, although these aspirations to have completely independent command of the knowledge needed to construct a light water reactor were deflated somewhat as the French government subsequently called for an "agreement of cooperation" to replace the previous licensing agreement.

Finally, firmer state control over the nuclear fuel cycle itself had become a top priority as demand for nuclear fuel increased rapidly. This led to the creation in 1976 of the CEA-affiliate Cogema (*Compagnie Générale des Matières Nucléaires*).

The prospecting and mining activities of Cogema, both within metropolitan France and overseas (primarily in Francophone Africa), soon began to show dividends. By the late 1970s, uranium production from French companies was sufficient to meet domestic needs and was expected to cover demand well into the future. In 1980, approximately 3,600 tons of uranium were required for French plants; domestic production met most of this (3,000 tons), while output from mines in which French companies had equity in Gabon, Niger, and Canada more than covered the difference (approximately 3,500 tons). Consumption is expected to peak at 10,000 tons around 1990, with production in France to reach 4,000 tons and mines in Gabon and Niger to supply the difference. In all, French companies claim to have secured about 240,000 metric tons of uranium—100,000 tons in France, 140,000 tons abroad.[5]

For its supply of enriched uranium, France had been dependent on the United States (and to a lesser degree on the Soviet Union) throughout the 1970s, but French efforts to develop and commercialize the gaseous diffusion technology began to bear fruit toward the end of the decade. Domestic requirements were increasingly being covered by production from Eurodif—a company in which France, Italy, Belgium, Spain, and Iran participate (with Iran withdrawing in 1980). The CEA (Cogema) holds the largest share, a little under one half. The first plant, located at Tricastin, was to reach its full capacity of 10,800 tons by the end of 1981; a second plant, to be built in stages but with an eventual capacity 10,000 tons, was planned for completion by 1988. The present worldwide surplus in enrichment capacity has resulted in its postponement.

In addition to prospecting, mining, and enrichment, Cogema has been active in the reprocessing of spent fuel at La Hague, despite persistent labor problems.

In short, French public officials responded to the energy crises of the 1970s with the rapid expansion of nuclear power, controlled and directed by the French state. It is not surprising that this strategy encountered considerable opposition within the country. But the small apparent impact of this opposition on the conduct of state policy requires further investigation.

OPPOSITION TO NUCLEAR POWER IN FRANCE

With the rapid industrial growth experienced in postwar France came the attendant problems of environmental pollution. As in most other advanced industrialized democracies, environmental concerns had begun to impinge on the political agenda in France by the early 1970s. Environmental groups had formed, organizations such as the Friends of the Earth, sociétés de protection de la nature, comités de défense de la Côte d'Azur, comités de défense de Bretagne (the 1967 Torrey Canyon oil spill was the first of a series of oil tanker accidents off the Brittany coast receiving international attention). Large protests had been held, such as the protests in 1973 against the construction of an expressway along the Left Bank of the Seine in Paris. Institutions responsible for environmental issues were created, such as the Ministry for the Protection of Nature and the Environment in 1971. Environmental legislation was initiated. Not until controversy over nuclear power erupted in 1974–75, however, did an environmental issue capture the sustained attention of high government officials.

Before the energy crisis, opposition to nuclear power, if it existed at all, was limited primarily to local communities where reactors were either under construction or planned. For example, local opposition to nuclear power had appeared as early as 1971 in protests at the Bugey plant. But with the government decision to accelerate the French nuclear program rapidly, the debate was taken up at the national level. By mid-1975, most important French newspapers had carried series of articles discussing questions of radioactivity, the risk of nuclear accident, the problems of nuclear waste, and the like.[6] In February 1975, just days after the announced decision to construct 12,000 MW over the next two years, a group of four hundred scientists declared their opposition to the government's nuclear program, at least until the risks and advantages of nuclear power could be more carefully assessed; they urged citizens "to refuse to accept the installation of nuclear reactors until they have a clear understanding of the risks and consequences . . . "[7] Protests sponsored by national, as well as local, anti-nuclear groups have multiplied since 1975; the largest and most violent, with a hundred injured and one killed, was a demonstration against construction of the FBR Super-Phénix at Creys-Malville in June 1977.

The French anti-nuclear movement showed several similarities with the one in West Germany during the mid-1970s. In both countries, protests started with local or regional groups, usually created on an ad hoc basis in response to the placing of a nuclear facility in the area. At the national level, these groups organized into loose networks with relatively few permanent members, but they were able to mobilize large numbers for special events. In West Germany, the most prominent national organization was the BBU (*Bundesverband Buergerinitiativen Umweltschutz*); in France, Les Amis de la Terre (Friends of the Earth). Anti-nuclear activists were generally young, well educated, and tended toward the left end of the political spectrum, although opposition to nuclear power extended well beyond these groups (see Table 12 in Appendix). Finally, in both countries, opposition to nuclear power within the general population increased during the mid-1970s. In France, support for nuclear power fell from 74 percent in 1974 to 47 percent in 1978; opposition increased from 17 percent to 42 percent. In West Germany, support declined from 60 percent in 1975 to 53 percent in 1977; opposition increased from 16 percent to 43 percent.[8]

There were, of course, differences as well. In France, for example, opposition to nuclear power has fused at times with a more general critique of the highly centralized French political system and demands for greater regional autonomy. Recent clashes between demonstrators and police in Brittany over the siting of a large nuclear plant with four 1300 MW reactors at Plogoff is illustrative of this: with little regard to the strong objections voiced by local authorities and the populace, Paris imposed this choice on the region.

The German anti-nuclear movement, in contrast, generally formulated its political positions much less ideologically, thereby hoping to avoid any association with radical forces in the country.[9] In the ability of nuclear opponents to affect actual policy, however, such differences were of little

consequence. The critical factor in this regard is the structure of the policymaking process itself.

NUCLEAR POLICY AND THE INSULARITY
OF THE FRENCH STATE

As is evident, the energy situations in France and the
Federal Republic during the 1970s were quite similar. Energy strategies in both countries placed initial emphasis on
the overriding importance of rapid nuclear power expansion
and an active anti-nuclear movement arose to contest this
expansion. In France, the initial government response to
this growing anti-nuclear movement was the creation of an
Information Council on Nuclear Energy (*Conseil de l'Information sur l'Energie Electronucléaire*), headed by Minister of
Health Simone Veil. As in West Germany, a public information campaign was initiated, on the assumption that
nuclear opposition was based primarily on insufficient or
inaccurate information. Subsequent provisions were made
for the Regional Assemblies to debate the location of new
nuclear plants. It was hoped that this would appease government critics and, at the same time, help to identify
potential sites least likely to encounter opposition.[10] The
latter objective may have been partially achieved; the
former was not. And finally, some flexibility was introduced
into the choice of sites. For example, if EDF met opposition
at a certain site, it would at times postpone further activity,
concentrating its efforts at sites where opposition was minimal.[11]

These largely tactical maneuvers, however, did little to
diffuse nuclear opposition. Demonstrations continued and
polls indicated the continuing unacceptability of nuclear
power to a sizable portion of the French population. As we
saw earlier, the polls found 47 percent for and 42 percent
against nuclear power in 1978; the Sofres/Le Matin polls
reported 56 percent for and 41 percent against in April 1981
and 65 percent for and 33 percent against in April 1982.[12]
Yet, except for the decision made in 1976 to cut back the

nuclear program from 12,000 MW to 10,000 MW for 1977–78, the French government had shown little inclination to slow down the nuclear program. Even this reduction was not due to the impact of nuclear opposition on the nuclear program but reflected the effects of slumping industrial activity, an anticipated slow economic recovery, and government support for the decision of the Finance Ministry to reduce somewhat the level of investment in the nuclear sector.

In other words, the French energy program has encountered few impediments sufficient to stall its execution, whereas efforts of the German government to implement major elements of its program have been continually thwarted. As we have seen, resistance in West Germany is not based on the availability of more attractive energy options. Compared to the United States or Great Britain, for example, Germany's dependence on imported oil is still relatively high; and the costs of extracting and processing German coal appear so great that extensive exploitation would be prohibitive. More compelling than differences in resources between the two countries are the differences in political structures and processes that either facilitate or inhibit the realization of government policy.

POLITICS AND THE POLICYMAKING PROCESS IN FRANCE

French political institutions have undergone considerable change since the Second World War. There has been one constant that has lent continuity to the political process, however—the French state. In the Fourth Republic, policymaking in general was characterized by the avoidance of any decision by government. The likelihood was very great that any important issue brought before the National Assembly would result in the fall of the current government; governments, therefore, avoided confrontations with parliament. Policymaking was carried out by abdicating significant power to the bureaucracy. Examples were numerous. In 1954, the government of Mendès France introduced the *loi-*

programme, which allowed planners "to draw on public funds for certain purposes independently of the annual budget."[13] Planning during the 1950s has been characterized as "voluntary collusion between senior civil servants and the managers of big business" in which government ministers and politicians, as well as organized labor and small business, were usually excluded.[14] And various plans important in setting post-war policy were "either never brought before Parliament, in the cases of the first and third plans, or considered by Parliament in conditions which made such consideration pointless (after the plan had been in effect for over two years) as with the second plan."[15]

Stanley Hoffmann has perhaps best summarized policymaking in the Fourth Republic:

> The Fourth Republic started with a major handicap. A multi-party system preserved by proportional representation had no chance of developing stable and coherent governments if problems to be dealt with prevented the formation of lasting majorities. . . . The regime established in 1946 . . . was gradually destroyed by its incapacity for dealing with issues. The problems of economic and social change were handled by the bureaucracy rather than by Parliament; what came before the nation's representatives were the incidents and crises in the process—budgetary or taxation difficulties, claims by special interests. In those cases, French parties . . . tended to behave more like pressure groups and to defend the interests of their principal voters. Their incapacity for defining coherent policy resulted in multiple cabinet crises and undermined the parliamentary system.[16]

With the return of Charles de Gaulle to political power in 1958, the executive reclaimed much of the control ceded by parliament during the Fourth Republic. The de facto impotence of parliament was transformed by the constitution of the Fifth Republic into de jure impotence as well. The role of the state bureaucracy in the policy process, however, was not similarly diminished. Although de Gaulle and those who subsequently occupied the office of President have exerted greater executive control through the Council of Ministers and various other high-level interministerial committees, the bureaucracy remains instrumental in the formulation as well as implementation of policies. This condition has been re-enforced by a practice which has accelerated during the Fifth Republic—one of bringing high-ranking administrators into the government itself.

We have seen how energy policy in the Federal Republic was greatly affected by the decentralizing forces of German federalism, with considerable judicial, administrative, and legislative power held at the Land level, by a stable parliamentary system featuring a constellation of parties competing for the political center, and by active, often effective, interest group participation in the political process. In the same way, nuclear policy in France has been shaped by the political features that, in many respects, are unique to the French system.

Energy policymaking from the late 1950s to the early 1970s has been described as follows: "With the exception of the first plan to decrease coal production (1958) and the abandonment of the French nuclear chain (1969), which gave rise to lively public reaction, policy making took place almost entirely among technocrats (high officials of the government and the administration and managers of public enterprises). Parliament was hardly consulted except to approve the plans, and the Council of Ministers resolved conflicts between administrations."[17]

In the wake of the energy crisis, the government appears to have assumed a more central role in energy policy, the final decision on all major elements of France's energy program having been taken within an interministerial council headed by the President. But this did not reduce the power of the bureaucracy appreciably: the issues had been discussed beforehand within such consultative committees as PEON, where the only serious challenge to the dominance of the CEA and EDF came from the Ministry of Finance. PEON was composed of the highest officials from the CEA and EDF, the three major *directions* of the Finance Ministry—Budget, Trésor, Direction de la Provision—the planning commission, representatives from major companies in the nuclear and oil sectors, and so forth.[18] This participation did not open the policy process to a greater range of opinion. Dissenting voices, especially any urging caution about the rapid expansion of nuclear power, have been conspicuously absent.

Opinion within the government and administration has uniformly held that a large nuclear program is indispensable for the security of France and that such a program poses no unacceptable environmental hazards. If any reservations were to be registered, one would expect them from the ministry responsible for environmental affairs, originally the Ministry for the Protection of Nature and the Environment, which, after several reshuffles, has been dubbed the Ministry for Culture and the Environment; but the ministry, being extremely low on the ministerial pecking order, has virtually no clout in the cabinet and, although it was eventually granted a seat on the PEON commission, its presence has largely been ignored by the other members.[19] The conflicts arising in the government over the nuclear program have been primarily over the rate of expansion, the prime example being the 1976 decision to cut back nuclear construction. It reflected the contrasting interests of the Ministry of Finance, which wanted to limit public investment, and EDF, which required massive amounts of capital for its construction program but was unable to acquire this money by means of self-financing because the government had granted electrical rate increases substantially lower than it had requested.

Throughout the 1970s, parliament too has remained far removed from the conduct of energy policy. The government's energy program wasn't even brought before the National Assembly until May 1975, where a perfunctory debate ensued. During the entire nine hours of discussion, no member seriously challenged the government's heavy reliance on nuclear power to meet France's future needs. In any case, the debate was more or less a formality: the day before, a member of the government majority in parliament had told *Le Monde* that "France's energy choices have already been made."[20] Nevertheless, at one point, the possibility was held out of a fundamental reevaluation of French energy policy, if the parliamentary elections held in March 1978 resulted in a change in government.

While the lack of real debate in the National Assembly to some degree reflected its lack of real power, it also was the result of a general consensus among virtually all political parties on the major thrust of French energy policy. Both major parties on the right—the Gaullists (RPR) and the Republicans (PR)—were strong advocates of nuclear power; and only minor points differentiated the parties on the left from their opposition. The reservations of the Communists (PCF) were limited to the government's preference for a "foreign" (American) technology, whereas the Socialists (PS) advocated greater diversification of energy supply and more energy conservation in order to allow the development of nuclear power "at a pace compatible with safety and energy requirements."[21] But this general agreement across the entire spectrum of France's party system left the concerns of nuclear critics unrepresented. Finding both the government and established political parties unresponsive to environmental concerns, ecologists formed their own parties in preparation for the municipal elections in March 1977. Precedent for environmentalist participation in the electoral process had been set in 1974 when, with the sponsorship of Les Amis de la Terre, René Dumont received almost 3 percent of the vote in the Presidential election.

With nuclear power an important issue in several regions of the country, the ecologists found a surprising degree of support, receiving over 10 percent of the vote. The ecologists were especially strong in Paris and the Paris region, receiving up to 15 percent in some arrondissements, as well as several large cities such as Mulhouse (13.7 percent), Grenoble (9.1 percent), and Lyons (8.6 percent). In the wake of their successes at the local level, they organized nationally in preparation for the parliamentary elections the next year.

The party most likely to be affected by the ecologists in the national election was the PS. According to a poll published in *Le Point* on September 1, 1977, ecologist voters were more likely to come from the left, specifically from the Socialists, than from the right, especially from the Gaullists. In addition, the CFDT—the second largest trade union in France, the largest union in the nuclear sector, and the one most closely aligned with the PS—was beginning to voice certain reservations about the government's nuclear program because of its concern about the working conditions of its members. Despite CFDT's overall support for nuclear power, the union took several actions. It had:

- Raised questions about the possible risks of rapid, large-scale nuclear expansion.[22]
- Staged a six-month strike at the La Hague reprocessing plant in an effort to force management to adopt more stringent safety standards.
- Demanded a three-year moratorium on the construction of new power plants.
- Opposed the expansion of reprocessing facilities at La Hague.
- Called on the government to refrain from signing new reprocessing contracts with other countries as well as cancel those already concluded.
- Sponsored a strike at the Gravelines reactor over the loading of the reactor ordered by EDF after small hairline fissures in the pipes had been discovered.

The largest trade union in France (the Communist CGT), on the other hand, remained a strong proponent of rapid nuclear power expansion.

Pressures to modify its stance on nuclear power began to mount within the PS; but the PS held its ground until the electoral alliance between it and the PCF broke down completely in September 1977. Pre-election polls had given the unified left a good chance of winning. It was also probable, however, that in the event of such a victory, the PS would become the largest party on the left—a condition unpalatable to the PCF, which had dominated the left throughout the post-war period. The occasion used to subvert the alliance was the negotiation of a common program. The PCF made demands totally unacceptable to the PS—specifically, the parties split over the issue of nationalization and the control of nationalized industries in a future government of the left. Following the breakdown, the PCF declared electoral war on the PS, often making Socialists rather than the parties of the right the object of its attack.

The Socialists now publicly re-evaluated their position on nuclear power. In October 1977, while still affirming general support for nuclear power, the PS called for an eighteen to twenty-four month moratorium on nuclear plant orders and the immediate suspension of construction on the Super-Phénix FBR.

In the wake of these developments, it was asserted that a "socialist success in the 1978 parliamentary election would probably lead to drastic modification of the nuclear program."[23] This was perhaps overstated, because the Socialists most likely would have had to govern in coalition with the Communists. The outcome of the March 1978 elections reduced such a discussion to idle speculation, however, as the Right won a majority of seats in the National Assembly on the second round of balloting, with the theme of anti-communism and stability dominating the last weeks of the campaign. In the first round, the Right received 48 percent of the vote as opposed to 49.7 percent by the Left—22.8 percent for the Socialist candidates, making the PS the largest single vote-getter but still far below the total anticipated. The Ecologists polled 2.1 percent. In the second round, however, the Right received 51.5 percent and the Left 48.5 percent, with no ecologist candidate surviving past the first round.

The presence of the ecologists did have some effect on the campaign. For one, they forced a discussion of environmental issues previously avoided or ignored by political parties in national elections. In addition, positions on energy policy within certain parties, most notably the PS, changed perceptibly when the ecologists entered the picture.

The poor showing of the ecologists, especially in contrast to the previous year's election results, indicated that environmental issues such as nuclear power were largely overshadowed by the traditional Left-Right dichotomy running through the French electorate. The major issues concerned each side's ability to cope with the problems of high unemployment, high inflation, and low economic growth.

In the Presidential campaign three years later, the Socialists and their candidate François Mitterand again voiced reservations about nuclear power. They charged that Giscard d'Estaing's concerted pushing of nuclear energy was imprudent. This stand attracted much of the ecologist vote and helped swing the final election to Mitterand. In the first round, Giscard d'Estaing received 28 percent, Mitterand 26 percent, and the environmental candidate, Brice Lalonde, 3.87 percent. In the second round, Mitterand, receiving most of the ecologist vote, polled 51.8 percent to Giscard's 48.2 percent. Yet, as we will see later, the Mitterand victory and subsequent election of a PS majority to parliament has not signaled a dramatic change in the course of nuclear policy.

Thus, unlike the situation in Germany, where the 5 percent clause enhanced the influence of the Greens, electoral politics in France offered little opportunity for nuclear opponents to affect the conduct of government nuclear policy. The electoral system and constellation of political parties in France served to dissipate the influence of the Ecologists. Of all the major parties, only the PS felt directly menaced by the ecologist vote, and this threat was diminished considerably by the two-round voting system.

THE LICENSING PROCESS

It was the same story in the other major area where anti-nuclear forces have been active, and in Germany quite successful: the licensing process for nuclear reactors. To say that nuclear licensing procedures in France have been unaffected by the anti-nuclear movement would not be accurate. We have already noted the government's decision to make public proposed plant sites where previously the choice and licensing of nuclear plants had occurred with little public discussion; and we have considered the flexibility demonstrated by EDF in the choice of sites. In addition, court appeals instigated by environmentalists after site approval have sometimes slowed the licensing process. Yet, despite such developments, the ability of the government to implement its nuclear program has remained unimpaired. Let us examine some of the reasons.

First, the vast majority of sites required to accommodate the rapidly accelerating nuclear program of the mid-1970s had been approved before the rise in anti-nuclear activity in 1975. Since most sites were planned to house four reactors, only nine sites were needed for the first thirty blocks constructed. When the government decided again to accelerate the nuclear program in 1979, one of the initial steps taken was the construction of two additional reactors at a site already approved and containing four plants.

Second, although the licensing process had slowed, no application for construction permits on new sites, as yet, has been denied. In contrast to the Federal Republic, France has a unified, central licensing procedure; the Ministry of Industry is the license-granting agency. Hearings are held at the site (*enquête locale*) where local officials, as well as affected individuals, have an opportunity to voice their opinion, although only in written form. The major participants, however, are always the same—EDF and Ministry of Industry officials—and, as a consequence, they have developed a well-practised routine.

Third, attempts by anti-nuclear groups to appeal the granting of certain construction permits have proved uniformly unsuccessful. There have been only two instances of administrative courts suspending construction permits—Flamanville, where several irregularities in the licensing process were discovered, and Belleville-sur-Loire, where the environmental protection report was ruled unsatisfactory.

The only avenue of appeal, however, leads directly to the Conseil d'Etat which, in both cases, lifted the construction stops within three to six months.

We can see that French energy officials have not had to deal with many of the forces that frustrated the efforts of their counterparts in the Federal Republic. They were spared the debilitating effects of intra-party—as well as federal-state—divisions. They were subjected to virtually no constraints by parliament, and they were able to neutralize efforts of environmental groups to impede implementation of the energy program. Consequently, French policymakers, confronted with a considerably less socially complex situation, showed little of the uncertainty that characterized German authorities. Rather than continual delays or postponements, the energy program was, if anything, marked by accelerated implementation. Rather than attempts to shift responsibility, strenuous efforts were made to guard policy prerogatives in the energy field. And rather than continual hedging on policy options, clear priority was given to rapid nuclear power development. In short, decisiveness characterized the response of French officials to domestic energy problems, a decisiveness underpinned and reinforced by a commonly held set of values or *Weltanschauung* among those in positions of political power.

THE ADMINISTRATIVE ELITE

Much has been written about the administrative elite who inhabit the highest offices of the French state and who, increasingly, have moved into government as well as industry.[24] Made up exclusively of members from the Grands Corps, it is an elite "united by a common educational background, common career horizons, and common corporate interests."[25] Membership in the Grands Corps is restricted to the very top graduates of either the Ecole Polytechnique (Corps des Mines, Corps des Ponts et Chausées) or ENA (Inspections des Finances, Cour des Compts, Conseil d'Etat). Most officials central to the formulation and implementa-

tion of energy policy in France came from this administrative elite: President Giscard d'Estaing, a graduate of both
Ecole Polytechnique (EP) and ENA, was an Inspecteur des
Finances; Minister of Industry André Giraud, former head of
CEA, was a graduate of EP and member of Corps des Mines;
the highest officials in CEA similarly graduate from EP and
belong to Corps des Mines; in EDF, EP and Corps des Ponts
et Chausées are the traditional career paths; and for the
Ministry of Finance it is ENA and Inspections des Finances.

Out of this milieu has emerged a distinctive view of the
state:

> The training . . . also has a moral objective. It is not
> one of the missions of the school [ENA] to play politics
> or to impose a particular doctrine. But the school must
> also teach its future civil servants "le sense de l'Etat",
> it must make them understand the responsibilities of
> the Administration, make them taste the grandeur and
> accept the servitudes of the metier.[26]

> The higher civil servants see themselves as represent-
> ing the general interest. . . . The State is the embodi-
> ment of the general interest; its purpose is to serve that
> general interest. . . . The hauts fonctionnaires act for
> the State and the State acts for the general interest. If
> their conception of what the general interest demands
> happens to clash with the views of some other groups,
> their job is to act, if need be over the objections of that
> group.[27]

> The elite believes that people rarely know what their
> long-term interests are. This clearly creates a gap
> which some members of society need to fill. Because the
> position it occupies and because of the way it came to
> occupy this position, the elite regards it as its duty to
> show the nonelite what its interests really are.[28]

These interests—when applied to energy policy—have
found expression in the protection of national "indepen-

dence," with nuclear power assigned a vital role in its maintenance. Whether articulated in relation to reducing French
dependence on imported fuel or maintaining the competitiveness and vitality of the French economy, the search for
national independence has been the underlying theme and
unifying rationale throughout the definition and execution
of French energy policy.[29] This has not meant that disputes
are unknown among the administrative elite who dominate
the policymaking framework. There was the conflict between EDF and CEA during the 1960s over the choice of
reactor types, the differences in the mid-1970s between the
Ministry of Finance and EDF over the rate of nuclear construction, and recent disputes between EDF and the CEA
over control of the sale and costs of uranium. Nevertheless,
officials have been unified in their response to criticism and
opposition from outside groups. Examples have been numerous.

In response to public concerns over nuclear safety after
the accident at Three Mile Island, the government simply
stated that such an accident was not possible in French
reactors, and then proceeded to accelerate the nuclear program. When controversy arose after hairline cracks were
found in the pipes of several reactors either under construction, in operation, or ready to be started up, EDF officials
maintained that these cracks did not constitute a serious
danger, although special monitoring procedures would be
set up for those reactors containing such pipes. In the cases
of the Tricastin and Gravelines reactors, where the CFDT
struck in response to EDF's unwillingness repair the cracks
before loading, the loading of the two reactors was carried
out despite the strikes.

To inquiries precipitated by the resignation of the Secre-
tary-General in the Inter-Ministerial Committee for Nuclear Safety because of obstruction by the Industry and
Health Ministries that prevented him from doing his job, the
government responded that there was nothing wrong with
the French safety system.[30]

Following initial efforts to keep quiet a fire at the La

Hague resprocessing plant in January 1981 in which several employees were contaminated by high-level radiation, officials reassured the public that the radioactivity that escaped was well within safety limits.

These reactions reflect the conviction held by French energy officials that nuclear power is less of a risk than other energy sources, that in any event some activities in modern society entail risk, and that fear of nuclear power is irrational and based primarily on poor information.[31]

Thus, the insularity built into the French political process, an insularity bred by the concentration of political power and the self-assured exercise of that power by a governing elite, has greatly simplified the execution of nuclear policy. This has not meant, however, that energy officials have been spared the strains and pulls of powerful competing interests. But the most notable decisions and events that have complicated the lives of those responsible for energy policy have come from outside the French polity.

ENERGY INDEPENDENCE, NUCLEAR POWER,
AND NON-PROLIFERATION

As we saw earlier, the rapid expansion of nuclear power, including concerted efforts to develop and integrate fully each phase of the nuclear fuel cycle, was part of an overall long-term design to reduce France's energy dependence. At the same time, however, these efforts were part of more immediate commercial and economic considerations associated with French industrial policy.

With the government decision to abandon its gas-graphite technology in favor of the LWR because of the former's poorer export prospects and the industrial restructuring necessitated by such a move, the French nuclear industry felt sufficiently well-placed to pursue foreign sales actively. By the mid-1970s, orders were beginning to come in; Framatome sold two LWRs to South Africa and Iran contracted for at least another two. In addition, research reactors were sold to Iran and Iraq; Pakistan and South Korea each had contracted for the construction of a reprocessing plant; and reprocessing services were becoming a major growth industry. Having invested approximately $1 billion to double the capacity of its La Hague plant, Cogema had received enough orders by 1979 to close its books through 1985. Among the customers contracting for reprocessing services were West Germany, Japan, Sweden, Switzerland, and the Netherlands.[32] Finally, France enjoyed a worldwide technological lead in development of the FBR with a 250 MW demonstration fast breeder reactor, the Phénix, in operation, the construction of the 1200 MW Super-Phénix prototype well underway and scheduled to go critical in 1985, and orders for two FBRs every three years expected from 1985 through the year 2000.[33] Expectations for the future commercial success of the French technology overseas were high.

Thus, the nuclear program not only represented deliverance from an untenable long-term dependence on foreign states, it contributed directly to the amelioration of certain economic problems confronting France, not the least being serious strains on the French balance of payments resulting from large oil imports. For these reasons, France was no more ready than was Germany for fundamental revisions of the rules and norms governing nuclear exports and the use of certain nuclear technologies.

Throughout much of the post-war period, French governments displayed little interest in the international regulation of nuclear proliferation (beyond the question of nuclear weapons for West Germany). France refused to sign the Nuclear Non-Proliferation Treaty, although it affirmed its support for non-proliferation provided that its domestic nuclear program remained unaffected.[34] Nevertheless, increased French activity both domestically and in the world market, in combination with a re-evaluation of non-proliferation policy precipitated by India's nuclear explosion, brought France into the vortex of a growing international debate over nuclear proliferation.

We have already discussed the international consultations among supplier countries—the so-called London Suppliers Group—on tighter safeguards and stricter nuclear export guidelines in the wake of events in India. The domestic effect of these discussions in France was to exacerbate relations within the coalition cabinet resulting, until summer 1976, in a near-paralysis of French nuclear export policy. For their part, the Gaullists, under the leadership of Prime Minister Chirac, opposed any attempt to revise France's policy, interpreting such efforts as acquiescence to American pressure. Not only had the United States spearheaded the initiatives in the suppliers group but also French nuclear export policy increasingly had come under pressure from the Ford administration. The sale of reprocessing facilities to South Korea and Pakistan, as well as the sale to Iraq of the research reactor that required highly enriched, weapons-grade uranium, were singled out for special criticism.

The supporters of President Giscard d'Estaing, on the other hand, apparently wished to exert firmer control over nuclear export policy but were for the most part thwarted by the Gaullist presence in government.[35] With the resignation of Chirac in August 1976, however, a series of measures were initiated by Giscard, signaling major revisions in French policy:

- On September 1, 1976, a council designed to formulate France's nuclear foreign policy (*Conseil Nucléaire de Politique extérieure*) was established under the chairmanship of the French President.
- Following the October 11, 1976, meeting of the Council, a communique was issued from the President's office laying out, in general terms, France's new foreign policy.
- On December 16, 1976, the Council issued an order to suspend the further export of reprocessing facilities.

The October communique said, in part:

France intends to keep control of its nuclear export policy with due respect for its international commitments in this field.

In its policy of nuclear exports France will strengthen all relevant regulations and guarantees in the field of equipment, materials and technology.

France will ensure safeguards for supplies of nuclear fuel for the nuclear power stations it provides and it will meet legitimate needs for access to technology. France will also furnish fuel-cycle services . . .

The French government is ready to discuss these problems with both the producer countries and the non-producer countries engaged in major programs for nuclear power stations.[36]

Thus, by the advent of the Carter administration, the central tenets of both French and American nuclear export policy appeared to be in basic agreement, although some differences remained. While French officials supported the tightening of safeguards, they opposed the "full-scope" safeguards being pushed by the United States; and in suspending the export of reprocessing plants, France did not preclude the export of sensitive technologies in the future. Certain issues also remained outstanding, such as the sale of the reprocessing plant to Pakistan. But once the French government had decided that the sale of the reprocessing facility to Pakistan was not in France's best interest, the primary task facing Giscard was how to stop delivery without appearing to cave in to U.S. pressures, which had again increased with the change of administrations. Refusing to abrogate the agreement unilaterally, French officials apparently hoped that, as in the case of South Korea, American pressures on Pakistan would result in the cancellation of the contract by the Pakistani government; the French government privately made clear that it wouldn't object to such actions. But Pakistan remained unmoved by the exhortations of the Americans and the hints of the French, adamantly demanding fulfillment of the agreement. The French government therefore took another tack, proposing a series of changes that, if adopted, would have resulted in long delays as well as significant alterations in the reprocessing process. Finally, in late 1978, the French government announced its decision to cancel the contract, a decision which by this time was met with considerable indifference by the Pakistanis. (This indifference is perhaps explained by the apparent success of an alternative strategy being pursued at the same time by Pakistan: the acquisition of an enrichment technology through industrial espionage by a Pakistani national employed for a time at the URENCO enrichment project in Almelo, the Netherlands.)

Another unresolved issue was the delivery of uranium enriched to 93 percent for the Osiris research reactor under construction in Iraq. In conjunction with France's newly enunciated non-proliferation policy, French government officials attempted to revise the agreement signed with Iraq in 1975. By 1980, however, the government had abandoned efforts to persuade Iraq to substitute a low-enrichment fuel being developed and tested in France (*caramel*, a fuel enriched to only 7–8 percent, substantially below the threshold for use in nuclear explosive device). Following the Israeli air strike against the Iraqi reactor, France and Iraq negotiated an agreement calling for the construction of a new reactor, but this time to be fueled by uranium enriched to around 20 percent, a much lower level than previously contracted for, although not the caramel earlier proposed.

It is not entirely clear how greatly the United States was responsible for this reorientation in France's export policy and for the efforts to revise the agreements with Pakistan and Iraq. The truth possibly lies somewhere between the position of Giscard's critics, the Gaullists, who maintained that he had acquiesced to American pressures, and that of his supporters, who naturally denied the influence of the United States, declaring that French nuclear export policy did not amount to an "alignment with Washington's views."[37] That is, U.S. exhortations probably had the greatest effect during the initial phase of the non-proliferation debate in 1974–76 by making explicit the implications of France's recently concluded nuclear export agreements; but these pressures, in and of themselves, were not sufficient cause, especially in view of the French tendency to resist foreign policy initiatives from across the Atlantic. Of equal or greater importance for changes in policy were certain domestic considerations that allowed French and American interests regarding the control of nuclear exports to come together. One such consideration was that the French did not see attempts to limit competition for export contracts as overly compromising of their interests, since the American and German nuclear industries, among others, were equally constrained by agreements reached within the suppliers group. Further, the need for foreign sales was not nearly so great for the French nuclear industry because of its rapidly expanding domestic market. Another consideration was that, with France's near-monopoly in the area of commercial reprocessing, the sale of reprocessing services to Third World countries was potentially much more lucrative than the export of such facilities. Reprocessing contracts concluded by Cogema earned approximately 12 billion francs in 1977 ($2.5 billion), whereas the contracts with South Korea and Pakistan totaled $10 million and $200 million respectively.[38]

Thus, shared concerns over the spread of nuclear weapons to politically sensitive areas of the Third World had developed into a general consensus that some controls had to be exerted over the export of nuclear technology. Nevertheless, French and American positions began to diverge sharply when, by 1977, new elements were introduced into the non-proliferation debate—the Carter administration's initiatives against plutonium-producing technologies.

Although the United States did not explicitly demand that other countries follow its lead in delaying indefinitely commercial reprocessing and deferring until later any decision on the commercialization of the FBR, the proposed discussion of the nuclear fuel cycle within an international framework (INFCE) and the subsequent passage by the U.S. Congress of the Nuclear Non- Proliferation Act of 1978 made clear the intention of the Carter administration to encourage similar actions by others. These policies, however,

struck directly at the heart of France's energy strategy,
threatening both its independence and economic viability.
Not surprisingly, the French vigorously defended the necessity of the fast breeder option and of reprocessing in unilateral declarations as well as in intergovernmental discussions through INFCE. Like their West German counterparts
(as detailed in Chapter 5), French officials argued that,
lacking the enormous energy reserves of the United States,
they were impelled to pursue early commercialization of the
FBR and the concomitant capture of plutonium through
reprocessing in order to significantly reduce France's dependence on imported oil. In addition, they emphasized that
reprocessing, aside from making much more efficient use of
energy resources, was ecologically sounder than long-term
storage of spent fuel rods: high-level radioactive waste could
be separated from the less hazardous material, solidified in
glass, placed in stainless steel containers, stored in concrete
pits, and then permanently isolated from the environment.
(As yet, no decision has been made on the method of final
disposal; under most serious consideration are burial in salt
domes, clay, or granite.)

The American policies posed lingering questions for the
viability of France's nuclear strategy, although, unlike the
German situation, the French strategy is not so dependent
on nuclear exports. The French nuclear industry actively
sought export business, but it could survive on domestic
orders. This contrasts with Germany, where international
sales were imperative because the domestic market had
virtually disappeared. Nor did the U.S. opposition to reprocessing and the FBR bolster the anti-nuclear forces in
France as they did in West Germany; policy in France was
in the hands of officials insulated from the pressures of
nuclear opponents.

The major problem posed for the French nuclear program
by the Carter administration's anti-plutonium crusade was
one of scale. If the United States were successful in persuad-
ing other major industrialized nations, as well as Third
World countries, to forego reprocessing and early commer-

cialization of the FBR, would such a program still be viable in a country the size of France? Further, despite France's being largely self-sufficient in enriched uranium by 1981, the United States retained some leverage over French reprocessing. Not only had a high percentage of enriched uranium been purchased earlier from the United States but most of the customers contracting for French reprocessing services at La Hague had been supplied primarily by the United States. In both instances, reprocessing was subject to American approval because of the NNPA.

As for the fast breeder reactor, analogies were inevitable with the Concorde supersonic airliner—a technological achievement but a commercial disaster, in part because the aircraft was excluded from major markets by the United States. French officials discount this comparison, but questions persist about the economic feasibility of the FBR in the absence of a larger market and with the possible loss of West Germany and other crucial partners in developing and marketing such an expensive and controversial technology. The government may have signaled its own doubts about economic feasibility: there are recent reports that plans to move beyond the Super-Phénix have been suspended until other nations assume more of the costs in research and application.[39]

THE NUCLEAR FUTURE IN FRANCE

As France entered the 1980s, two questions hovered over the political landscape, clouding the otherwise optimistic future of its nuclear program. The first question concerned the international debate over nuclear proliferation and its possible effect on domestic policy options; the second related to the role of nuclear power under a Socialist government. Subsequent developments, however, indicate little threat from either source.

The findings at INFCE, as we saw in the previous chapter, combined with a new American administration more favorably disposed to reprocessing and development of the FBR, have reduced potential constraints on nuclear power from external sources.

In the domestic arena, initial measures undertaken by the new Socialist government in 1981 raised concerns among proponents of nuclear power. The controversial Plogoff plant was canceled outright, construction on five other reactors was frozen, and a general debate was initiated over the future direction of French nuclear policy. Under discussion were the rate of construction on new nuclear power plants, the future of the FBR, and the expansion of the reprocessing plant at la Hague. But once the debate was concluded in October 1981 with a parliamentary vote, little had changed in the fundamental direction and content of French nuclear policy:

- Six new LWRs would be ordered over 1982–83 rather than the nine planned by the previous government over the same period. This rate of expansion has not been realized because of forecasts of lower increases in energy demand and projections of at least 13 percent excess generating capacity by 1990; for 1983–84, a cutback from three to two reactors per year was ordered; for 1985–86, one per year.[40]
- By 1990, the share of domestic energy consumption to be covered by nuclear power was set at 27 percent, down only slightly from the 30 percent projected in the 1980 program of Giscard.
- The Super-Phénix FBR was to be completed, with a decision on starting a series of FBRs to be reserved for later.
- Reprocessing capacity was to be expanded.

Thus, despite considerable public opposition to nuclear power through the 1970s, recent significant changes at the highest levels of government, and the growing prospect of surplus electrical generating capacity by the end of the decade, the French nuclear program, although slowing down owing to lower demand, has continued on course with only slight shifts in emphasis. This is perhaps a testimony to the structure of the policymaking process in France and the more persistent and powerful position of state agencies and their officials in that process.

7. Consensus Politics in the Netherlands

As our examinations of French and German energy policies have demonstrated, a country's response to recent dramatic shifts in the world energy market is not governed only by its indigenous energy resources but by political, economic, and social factors as well. Dutch policy, as we would expect, reflects a unique combination of elements present in the Netherlands.

As in France, a sophisticated state planning apparatus has been developed in the Netherlands to influence various economic activities; in addition, ownership of major energy sources is shared by the public and private sectors. As in West Germany, government intervention in the market-place has been quite limited and very discreet throughout much of the post-war period despite the presence of planning and public ownership. Moreover, the parliamentary system of government has remained remarkably open and stable, despite long-enduring and deep-seated divisions within Dutch society. It is most strikingly Dutch that, despite these divisions, public officials have traditionally placed a premium on achieving a broad political consensus in the policymaking process.[1] In the following pages, we will assess the effect of this rather exceptional combination of factors on the shaping of nuclear policy in postwar Holland.

GOVERNMENT NUCLEAR POLICY

In fall 1974, an energy White Paper was submitted by the Ministry of Economic Affairs to parliament, a major component of which was nuclear power. (For the composition of the government at this time, see Chapter 3.)

The report cited the various benefits to be derived from the introduction of nuclear power—diversification of energy supplies, a less expensive means of generating electricity, beneficial effects on employment, favorable impact on the country's balance of payments, slower depletion of the Slochteren natural gas field, and the absence of air pollution—and proposed a gradual expansion of nuclear energy. To be more precise, the construction of three 1,000 MW reactors was to be completed by 1985. With the inclusion of two reactors already operating whose combined output was 500 MW, this would represent 20 percent of the Netherlands' electricity.

Following publication of the Economic Ministry's White Paper, it was decided to make this proposal conditional on the completion of several studies covering health, siting, and safety aspects of nuclear power. The Ministries of Economic Affairs, Public Health and Environment, and Social Welfare and Employment were subsequently commissioned to carry out these studies; and by fall 1975, the reports had been completed.[2]

Interpreting the studies as permitting the planned expansion of nuclear power, Economics Minister Lubbers proposed the expansion of nuclear capacity by 3,000 MW in October 1975. As in both West Germany and France, public opposition to nuclear power began to build. In contrast to both other countries, however, adoption by the Council of Ministers, let alone approval by parliament, increasingly appeared problematic.

A CALL FOR REFLECTION

The nationwide debate over nuclear energy largely began in 1974 with publication of the White Paper. The seeds of opposition in the Netherlands were planted by the Reflection Group on Energy Policy (*Bezziningsgroep Energiebeleid*), a small group of between twenty and thirty members composed of prominent journalists, members of parliament, and scientists, including several from industry. Believing that the White Paper contained serious shortcomings, the group prepared a "reflection" paper highly critical of the Economic Ministry's analysis of the proposed nuclear program. The group charged that the risks to population or the environment were not given sufficiently serious discussion. It faulted the failure to make any socio-economic quantification of the alternatives to nuclear power and the avoidance of any clear articulation of socio-economic priorities, other than becoming less dependent on the oil producers. Although the group did not present an alternative energy program, its paper did recommend a five-year reflection period to reconsider the Netherlands' energy future. In the following year, responding to Minister Lubbers's move to seek cabinet approval for the nuclear program in October 1975, the group published a Second Reflection Paper, again arguing that a period of reflection was necessary for careful analysis of other options—which, in contrast to the first paper, were now discussed in considerable detail.[3]

The Reflection Group was among the first, the most articulate, and most highly publicized groups to voice concerns over the nuclear program. The First Reflection Paper, for example, was released at a press conference scheduled to coincide with the discussion of the White Paper in the Council of Ministers. Receiving considerable attention in the mass media, it was even given credit for a delay in the official publication of the energy paper (evidently, an earlier draft had been leaked to members of the Reflection Group). Similarly, just before the February 1976 cabinet meeting where a final decision on the nuclear power program was to be made, an abstract of the Second Reflection Paper was made into a full-page advertisement paid for and signed by 1,200 concerned scientists, which appeared in several major newspapers. The most prominent among them were Professor Casimir, President of the Dutch Royal Academy of Science and President of the European Physicists Society; Dr. Beck, Managing Director and Research Coordinator of Unilever; Professor Tinbergen, Nobel Laureate in Economics; Dr. Mansholt, former President of the European Commission; and Professors Schillebeeckx and Verkuyle, well-known Roman Catholic and Dutch Reformed theologians.

The Reflection Group was not alone in its opposition to nuclear power. The debate was soon joined by various other organizations, both public and private, throughout the country. Cities and provinces designated as possible sites for nuclear reactors came out publicly in opposition to the construction of nuclear power plants in their districts. In 1974, the provincial council of South Holland voted 42 to 19 for a resolution expressing regret that the provincial executive supported plans of the SEP to construct a nuclear plant near Rotterdam; it said that it was not yet desirable for such a plant to be built because the safety of the population and the environment was not sufficiently guaranteed. In January 1975, the city council of Rotterdam passed a resolution, 23 to 1, declaring that under no condition should a nuclear power plant be built on a proposed industrial site near the city.

Trade union organizations gradually took positions opposing the nuclear program, demanding a five-year moratorium on the expansion of the nuclear power sector. The central organ for the three largest unions had published an "alternative" energy report in 1975, although the protestant labor union later issued a statement that supposedly undermined the effect of the report.[4] Nevertheless, by 1977–78 all major trade unions in Holland appeared to be in general agreement in their opposition to nuclear power, with the FNV—a federation of the Socialist NVV and Roman Catholic NKV, representing 80 percent of organized labor—again declaring in September 1977 that the expansion of nuclear power must be delayed, and the protestant CNV expressing considerable reservations about the further construction of nuclear power plants.[5]

Finally, several political parties belonging to the governing coalition increasingly distanced themselves from the proposed expansion of nuclear power. The most adamant in its opposition was the PPR; although small, this left-wing party was crucial to maintaining the coalition. More significantly, many of the leading members of the largest party in parliament, the PvdA, were vigorously opposed to nuclear power. Once out of government, the entire Labor Party came out strongly against any nuclear expansion.

Thus, while nuclear power enjoyed the official sanction of the Ministry of Economic Affairs, major political, social, and economic groups were increasingly opposed to the Ministry's nuclear program. Equally significant was the hesitation within government as well: after threats of resignation by two ministers, the government announced in February 1976 that a decision on nuclear power would be postponed until after the parliamentary elections scheduled for May 1977. The final vote within the cabinet reportedly was close to a deadlock; and while it is difficult to gage the actual impact of the public debate on the outcome, it was noted that at least two members of the Council of Ministers—F.H.A. Trip (PPR), Minister of Science, and Irene Vorrink (PvdA), Minister of the Environment—were in close contact with the Reflection Group throughout the cabinet deliberations. Perhaps more telling, however, was the Economic Affairs Minister's having to respond in detail during cabinet meetings to questions that had been raised by the Reflection Group.

The postponement averted an immediate government crisis, because the formation of a new coalition would have been virtually impossible with the party divisions then present within parliament. The longer-term effect, however, was a delay that extended well beyond the May 1977 elections, although the elections brought the VVD into the government in coalition with the CDA—parties much more favorably disposed toward nuclear power than were the PvdA and the PPR.

In deferring a final ruling on nuclear power until after an election over a year away, the cabinet acknowledged the substantial influence of the well-orchestrated nuclear oppo-

sition, bolstered by a general lack of enthusiasm for nuclear
power within the public at large. In a 1974 public opinion
poll, 58 percent opposed an immediate start of nuclear power
development, up from 35 percent in 1973; and 62 percent
believed that the technology was not yet able to guarantee
safe use.[6] The Second Reflection paper reported in 1975 that
54 percent of the public had expressed opposition to nuclear
power. A 1980 poll showed public opposition continuing
high, with 53 percent of those polled speaking against nuclear energy.[7] And, unlike West Germany with its powerful
industrial interests, the Netherlands had no strong nuclear
proponents to balance public doubt; such support as there
was came primarily from the SEP, parts of Dutch industry,
and the Ministry of Economic Affairs itself.

The delay on a final ruling was also a strategy to defuse
controversy over the nuclear issue in order to construct the
broad-based consensus customarily sought in Dutch politics.
Rather than gaining respite by the decision to defer judgment on the nuclear program, however, Dutch policymakers
remained embroiled in nuclear controversy over the next
few years, largely because of the association of virtually all
important nuclear-related industrial activities in Holland
with international programs.

NUCLEAR POWER AND THE
INTERNATIONAL NUCLEAR DEBATE

The size of the Dutch energy market and the amount of
funding required for independent development of competitive advanced reactor types more or less dictated the options
available to the Dutch government. It could either participate in international projects or remove the Netherlands
from any future commercial activities in the advanced reactor area. The Dutch government chose the former.

In 1967, the Netherlands, through its principal nuclear
firm, Neratoom, joined the German fast breeder project at
Kalkar. At the time, the action received little public attention, but by 1973 controversy surrounded the project. The

trigger was the so-called Kalkar Surtax—a 3 percent levy on all electrical bills to finance the Dutch participation. Thousands of individuals refused to pay the tax, with over seventy municipalities declaring their unwillingness to hand over the 3 percent that they had collected on electrical bills if the money went to Kalkar. Several groups—especially the trade unions, particularly NVV—called for the termination of Dutch participation in the project.

Economics Minister Lubbers made a hurried attempt to defuse the issue by allowing diversion of the 3 percent tax on individuals' utility bills to a special fund for the development of alternative energy sources if the person declared a conscientious objection to supporting the Kalkar project.[8] This ploy failed, however, as pressures for withdrawal from the Kalkar project mounted. More significantly, the antipathy to Kalkar began to fuse with the general opposition to the nuclear program proposed by the Ministry of Economic Affairs.

Despite the pressures, the government remained resolute in its intention to stay in the program, arguing that withdrawal would result in the payment of extremely high damages to its German and Belgian partners. A modus vivendi was finally reached in 1976 when, in conjunction with a governmental declaration renouncing participation of the Netherlands in a projected second phase of the Kalkar project, parliament approved a government proposal to abolish the Kalkar Fund on January 1, 1977. During 1976, the controversy over FBR development also was aggravated by the decision of SEP to join the French Super-Phénix project.

Participation in the Super-Phénix project was particularly attractive to Dutch authorities as they didn't have to take part in the financing of the "unprofitable top." In addition, Minister Lubbers held that if the Netherlands didn't participate, Holland would be kept outside FBR development, thereby diminishing the possibility that Dutch industry would be able to export nuclear reactor components. As a consequence, Lubbers instructed the Ministry's representative on SEP's board to approve the plan, which translated into an expenditure of Fl 23 million. This decision encountered strong opposition in parliament, the VVD being virtually the only party to back the Minister's move. Consequently, the Second Chamber passed a resolution which required that cooperation in the Super-Phénix project be made contingent upon the right of co-decision on safety requirements—requirements relating to guarantees against proliferation of nuclear materials and know-how as well as internal safety. In September 1976 the SEP board of directors approved the proposal for participation but stipulated that the construction of Super-Phénix should be subject to European Community safety requirements and that fissionable material used or produced by the reactor should be duly supervised.

The second area of dispute to feed the fires of nuclear controversy before the 1977 elections involved the export of nuclear reactors to South Africa. In spring 1976, an international consortium composed of GE, Brown-Boveri, and the Dutch group Rijn-Schelde-Verlome was chosen to build two nuclear reactors in South Africa. The project represented nearly Fl 1 billion in sales and approximately 5,000 jobs for a year; the Dutch government was asked to provide export credit facilities. While the left of center parties, along with the unions, strongly opposed the deal, the confessional parties favored the extension of export credits, maintaining that the guarantee and apartheid were two entirely separate questions. The dispute, however, never reached the floor of the Second Chamber.

Division within the cabinet ran very deep; resignations had been threatened both if credits were approved and if they were refused, so that any ruling threatened dissolution of the governing coalition and the fall of the government. The cabinet therefore repeatedly postponed a decision although South Africa had specified a deadline of May 21, 1976. With passing of the deadline, the outcome that the government leaders probably wanted was produced: South Africa awarded the contract to a French consortium, removing this extremely divisive issue from the Dutch political agenda.

During the course of 1976, the officials in the Netherlands had made every effort to depoliticize the nuclear question. They had postponed consideration of domestic nuclear power expansion indefinitely; Dutch participation in FBR development, although not terminated, had been substantially regulated; and the dispute over nuclear exports to South Africa dissipated quickly after government procrastination had lost the contract. But just when the issues fueling the nuclear controversy seemed to have been taken off the political agenda, the international debate over nuclear proliferation flared, spilling over into the domestic arena. The Dutch government was caught up in the debate because of the delivery of enriched uranium to Brazil.

The Netherlands had become directly involved in the controversy over the German-Brazilian deal because of its participation in Urenco, an enrichment project founded in 1971 with the Federal Republic of Germany, Great Britain, and Holland. Included in the German agreement with Brazil was a provision for the supply of enriched uranium from Urenco facilities located at Almelo in the Netherlands. In July 1976, the Dutch government approved the export to Brazil of uranium enriched by Urenco, but this decision increasingly came under fire from domestic critics concerned about the implications of such deliveries to a country that had refused to sign the Non-Proliferation Treaty.

Linked to the export of enriched uranium to Brazil was the planned expansion of the productive capacity at the Almelo plant. By 1982, approximately Fl 700 million was to be invested by the Netherlands through UCN (*Ultracentrifuge Netherlands*), the state-owned company originally composed of the Dutch government, with a 55 percent share, and five private companies, among them Philips and Shell, each with 10 percent. In October 1976, the companies terminated their financial participation in UCN. This made it into a totally state-owned company, requiring the government to come up with the entire Dutch share of the amount to be invested in the expansion of Almelo. Subsequently, the Labor party hinged its approval of Urenco enlargement on a "satisfactory" solution of the Brazilian supply question; the PPR opposed deliveries to Brazil altogether. It therefore opposed plans to expand Almelo.

In December 1976, the question came to a head in the Dutch cabinet when ministers from the PPR threatened to resign if expansion of Almelo were approved. The other government parties were at least reservedly in favor of expansion, because of the danger of losing as many as 2,000 jobs at the Almelo plant and because they felt that expansion would allow greater influence over the use of uranium enriched by Urenco and thereby restrict the spread of nuclear weapons. The cabinet met the dilemma by provisionally agreeing to expansion but with certain conditions attached. Final consent would be contingent on discussion by the Foreign and Economics Ministers with their German and British counterparts on various financial, organizational, and economic questions; and on guarantees governing supplies by Urenco to other countries in the interest of non-proliferation. This meant that Brazil must agree to international and IAEA controls.

In January 1977, at the PvdA congress held in preparation for the parliamentary elections in May, the party adopted a position very close to that of the PPR and that directly contradicted the policy of the Labor ministers in the cabinet: expansion of the Almelo plant was to be opposed. In the subsequent months leading to and following the national elections, little progress was made toward resolving the question. But with the formation of a new government in December 1977, agreement within the cabinet finally seemed possible: the VVD was a strong supporter of expansion and the confessional parties, now consolidated into the CDA, had favored approval, even if more conditionally.

In January 1978, Brazil exchanged letters with the three Urenco partners. It was agreed that all four countries would try to negotiate the establishment of a worldwide plutonium storage system run by the IAEA or, if this proved impossible, to negotiate on their own an ad hoc storage regime, again including the IAEA. Deciding that this commitment by the Brazilian government was sufficient, the new cabinet decided to go ahead with the enlargement of Almelo. But parliament, in voting for expansion, again attached conditions. Left-wing members of the CDA, supported by the Labor party now in opposition and staunchly opposed to expansion, stipulated that delivery of uranium to Brazil, scheduled to begin in 1981, would be permitted only if satisfactory safeguards had been worked out in the interim. The so-called van Houwelingen motion—named after one of the rebel CDA members in parliament—committed the Dutch government to "persuade" its Urenco partners and Brazil to complete nuclear safeguard negotiations by 1981, whereas the exchanged letters permitted negotiations to last until 1985 when uranium delivery and reprocessing were scheduled to begin.

Not surprisingly, little success followed from the efforts of the Netherlands to pry further concessions from German and British officials, who were increasingly exasperated by the long delays and seemingly unending demands for revisions. The German government made clear that it was not prepared to provide funds for the extension of the Almelo plant on the basis of the van Houwelingen amendment and threatened more extreme actions. Chancellor Schmidt warned in April 1978 that failure to observe contractual commitments would lead to "extremely stiff penalties."[9] The German and British partners let it be known that Brazil would be supplied, regardless of Dutch opposition. The uranium could come either from the British enrichment plant at Capenhurst or from new facilities being considered in Germany. German government officials had announced the possible early construction of enrichment facilities if the Dutch continued to delay; relatedly, the German partner in the Urenco consortium applied for a government permit to build an enrichment plant at Gronau. Further, there were hints that the Netherlands would be excluded from further participation in Urenco if the Dutch were not interested in a "further intensification of cooperation" in the area of enrichment.[10]

In June 1978, parliament finally agreed to the export of enriched uranium to Brazil, following a three-day debate in which the government argued that continued opposition would not improve the conditions of delivery to Brazil but would only result in the exclusion of Dutch industry from the Brazilian deal at the cost of thousands of jobs tied to the Almelo plant. The maverick CDA members relented in the end, although they did manage to extract one concession from the Prime Minister: the Second Chamber would be able to review the export permit in 1981 to determine whether, according to its members, the existing security guarantees were sufficient.

Thus, despite considerable opposition, the Netherlands continued to participate in the various multinational arrangements involving FBR development and the export of nuclear materials. The sale of reactors to South Africa was one exception. Nevertheless, the effect of the opposition should not be minimized. The questions raised by Dutch participation in these projects operated to sustain the domestic controversy over nuclear power at a time when the government was attempting to place the nuclear issue on the political back burner.

THE UNENDING SEARCH FOR CONSENSUS

Reflecting the continuing reservations in the country about nuclear power, the government that was formed in December 1977—although more favorably disposed to nuclear expansion than its predecessor—announced that the construction of new nuclear power plants would not be considered until certain problems related to nuclear energy had been satisfactorily resolved, among them the storage of nuclear waste and reactor safety. This decision was taken despite a projected increase in oil consumption—as much as

47 percent of primary energy demand by the mid-1980s, up from 41 percent in 1978.

Only after a prolonged hiatus extending over several years were the next tentative steps taken toward a political decision on the longer-term direction of Dutch energy policy. In the course of 1980 two government White Papers on energy policy were published by the Ministry of Economic Affairs.

The first memorandum, released in February 1978, recommended a dramatic increase in coal use as one element of the government's strategy to diversify Dutch energy supplies over the next decades.[11] Coal consumption was to approach 26 million tons per year by the year 2000 (up from the current level of 1.5 million tons), which would represent 40 percent of electricity production and 20 percent of total energy requirements (both currently at 5 percent). Reflecting this general commitment to greater coal use, the two power plants under construction in 1980 were coal-burning, with approximately 2500 MW of coal-fired capacity slated for construction after 1986.[12] Yet, despite such increases, the overall target advanced in the White Paper—a decline in the share of oil and gas from the current 90 percent of total energy needs to 20 percent by 2000—could not be approached without further diversification or considerably higher levels of coal consumption.

The second government White Paper, appearing in July 1980, specified nuclear power as the preferred alternative. It concluded that nuclear power was environmentally neither more nor less advantageous than coal and that nuclear waste could be safely stored above ground pending the construction of disposal facilities either underground or on the seabed. Accordingly, it proposed that parliament approve the construction of three nuclear power plants, so that 40 percent of electrical production would come from nuclear power in the year 2000.

The Second Chamber, however, was not to act immediately on the revived proposal for nuclear power expansion;

the final decision was to come only after an extensive two- to three-year public inquiry into the energy options contained in the White Papers. As in West Germany, the issue of increased nuclear power generation became linked with the question of nuclear waste management, any expansion being made contingent on finding a practical solution to the disposal problem. Salt domes in the northern provinces of Groningen and Drenthe were considered the most likely means of disposal, but local opposition has been so strong that parliament forbid exploratory drillings pending the outcome of the public debate on nuclear energy.

In the intervening years, there had been a quick succession of governments, each holding differing degrees of commitment to nuclear energy. The government established after the May 1981 election—a left of center coalition consisting of the PvdA, CD, and D'66—appeared much less favorably disposed to nuclear power: within six months of its entering office in September 1981, a report was to be made on the possible consequences of a closure of the two nuclear plants currently operating in the Netherlands. Over the next several months, however, the coalition collapsed twice, necessitating a new election in September 1982. The results eventually led to the return of a CD/Liberal coalition, this time under the leadership of Rudi Lubbers, former Minister of Economic Affairs and, as such, author of the 1974 White Paper. In January 1984, results of the extended public inquiry were submitted to the Economics Ministry. The report was based on approximately 42,000 questionaires filled out by participants at over 3,000 meetings, as well as on more representative polls of the general public. Among the findings:

- A vast majority of the population opposed further nuclear expansion.
- Only a small majority supported the continued operation of the two existing nuclear power plants.
- A large minority favored a complete withdrawal from nuclear power.

Accordingly, the report called for no further nuclear power

plants, as well as limits on the expansion of coal-burning plants. At the same time, the report recommended an ambitious program of energy conservation and development of renewable energy sources as an alternative. Along with the strong opposition to nuclear power, the study found little public support for coal, which was considered dirty, or for oil, which was believed too expensive and was controlled by foreigners. About the only energy source finding widespread support throughout the Dutch populace was windmills.[13]

POLICY PARALYSIS

Nuclear policy in the Netherlands is very much the product of a relatively open political system that places a premium on the widest possible consensus. It is clear from events of the past decade that the political uncertainties surrounding nuclear power have made a workable consensus on the nuclear issue nearly impossible to achieve.

The publication of the energy White Paper in 1974 and subsequent initiatives by the Economics Ministry to expand the nuclear program did not draw the desired support. Rather, they alerted diverse groups in the Netherlands to government involvement that directly affected such highly valued interests as environmental preservation, economic growth and welfare, and the possible spread of nuclear weapons. As a result, pressures mounted from local governments, from important parts of the trade union movement, and from environmental groups. Opposition also came from a majority of the general public, from prominent scientists and theologians, and from certain political parties as well as from divisions within others. This negative consensus has left the government paralyzed. No government, regardless of the combination of political parties in the often delicately balanced coalitions, has felt in a position even to place the nuclear program before parliament. The findings from the most recent public inquiry make the likelihood of renewed government initiatives in the nuclear sector extremely remote.

8. Nuclear Politics and Policymaking

In contrast to early expectations of government leaders in West Germany, France, and the Netherlands, the controversy over nuclear power has not been the transitory phenomenon once hoped for. Reassurances concerning the safety of nuclear power notwithstanding, the issue has remained central to the energy debate for a decade. Explanations for the concerns over nuclear power most commonly focus on the nature of the technology itself and the fears it engenders. The release of low-level radiation is part of the normal operation of the reactor; there is the possibility of a large-scale accident; heat released from the plant impacts on the surrounding environment; difficulties are inherent in the permanent disposal of highly radioactive waste; and the creation of a plutonium economy has implications for nuclear proliferation.

Further, observers have found explanations for the continuing controversy in certain aspects of building and operating nuclear power facilities that are difficult for modern political procedures to manage. Because of the long lead times involved in the construction of plants, the huge requirements of capital and expertise, and the extensive government involvement in development and regulation of the technology, nuclear power now embodies many of the problems of advanced, industrialized societies—rapid technological change, centralization of decision-making power, the intrusion of government bureaucracy.[1]

There can be little doubt that such factors are important in any explanation of the nuclear controversy. The foregoing studies of German, French, and Dutch energy policies, however, suggest the presence of an additional element. This element is not related directly to nuclear power but rather to the overall strategy used in the formulation of energy policy. More specifically, as political units move from a more limited, ad hoc approach to energy policy that relies primarily on the market to a comprehensive, long-term energy strategy in which government plays a more central role, the nuclear controversy changes from a scattered, localized phenomenon to a national debate that engages the major political, social, and economic institutions of the country. A brief explication of certain paradigms in the literature on decision-making may suggest why.

The more limited, market-oriented approach that typified energy policy in the 1960s corresponds closely to what organization theory would call "disjointed incrementalism."[2] When considered in relation to an alternative decision-making strategy—labeled "synoptic" or "rational-analytic"—disjointed incrementalism is characterized, among other things, by

- The blurring of means and ends rather than the explicit separation of objectives and the means to achieve those objectives.
- A disaggregated, limited, reactive approach to the analysis of a problem rather than a comprehensive approach in which every relevant factor is taken into account (often with the aid of systems analysis, cost-benefit analysis, and the like).
- The reliance on empiricism based on a succession of similar comparisons rather than on "theory," or the production of "theoretical" information (which is necessitated by comprehensive demands for information and analysis).

The advantages attributed to the trial-and-error method, or "muddling through," derive largely from its being the way

that the political process actually works. "Muddling
through" acknowledges the limited human capacity for comprehensiveness; intellectual capabilities are only finite and
it is impossible to possess total information. There is also an
important normative argument made for incrementalism,
however. That is, it reduces conflict and keeps social cleav-
ages to a minimum, thus facilitating agreement on policy
decisions. This is done in three ways. First, whereas an
explicit separation of fact and value—means and ends—
exacerbates disagreement over policy, the fusion of means
and ends disposes the various parties to consensus. Second,
the remedial nature of incrementalism avoids many difficulties raised by the formulation of long-term goals. It is
often much easier for differing parties to agree on situations
or ills that they wish to avoid or remedy than on goals
toward which to move. Third, increments of change reduce
the areas where social disagreement is possible. When only
politically relevant issues are considered, the parties avoid
additional differences over extraneous issues that are often
brought to the surface by demands for comprehensiveness.

Incrementalism, hoever, has not been without its detrac-
tors. At least three general critiques have been leveled at
the incrementalist strategy of decision making. First, it has
difficulty in responding to situations of rapid change. Second, its short-term orientation often leads to stagnation,
drift, or possibly exacerbation of problems. Third, it tends to
permit powerful groups within the system to exercise dis-
proportionate influence on the decision-making process.[3] It
should perhaps be noted that the market, as metaphor, has
served as a major source for the theoretical assumptions
underpinning the incremental strategy. Responsibility is
widely dispersed, fragmented, and decentralized, with ag-
gregate public welfare resulting from the pursuit of narrow
self-interests. Similarly, many of the critiques of the market
parallel those of incrementalism. Monopoly positions develop in the market, which cause serious distortions in the
economy; "externalities" have resulted from the inability of

the market to reflect certain costs; and short-range goals are often pursued to the neglect of the future.

In any event, to the strategy of disjointed incrementalism has been ascribed the ability to minimize social conflict. To do this would be no insignificant accomplishment, in view of the complex problems confronting advanced industrial societies today. Regardless of the virtues of incrementalism, however, the foregoing case studies have illustrated the efforts of policymakers in three countries to deal with a myriad of interlinked energy-related problems by means of a more synoptic, comprehensive energy strategy.

In West Germany throughout much of the post-war period, energy policy mirrored many of the characteristics of incremental decision making. Policy was limited in scope, being primarily concerned with the coal sector; it was remedial in nature, being designed to ameliorate the problems of the declining coal sector; and it was reliant on a trial-and-error approach, taking the market as final arbiter. By the mid-1970s, this approach to energy issues had undergone fundamental transformation. Policy proposals were now largely anticipatory rather than remedial, government intervention in many areas associated with energy supply was now the rule rather than the exception, attempts at comprehensive analysis had displaced empiricism as the basis of policy choice, and political objectives had become very comprehensive in nature.

In France, the pattern of energy decision making diverged in certain respects from the German experience. In the years immediately following the Second World War, French energy policy represented a limited rational-analytic approach. Planning in the energy sector, although lacking a certain degree of comprehensiveness and more medium- than long-term in nature, manipulated or restricted the market from prejudicing energy policy objectives; this was accomplished through pervasive state intervention—for example, the development of national, but more expensive, energy resources. But as France's economy began to open up with the creation of the Common Market, policymaking became more incremental as increasingly it began to rely on that most incremental of policy instruments, the market. While the state remained extremely active in the energy sector, its activities were guided less by a "plan" than by developments in the international energy market. With the international competitiveness of French industry supplanting energy independence as the major concern of public officials, market forces increasingly dictated the patterns of French energy consumption throughout the 1960s.

The effects of rapidly rising energy consumption throughout the 1960s, when combined with dramatic changes in the structure of the world energy market during the early 1970s, precipitated a fundamental reorientation of French energy policy. Instead of pursuing international competitiveness through reliance on the international oil market, public officials began to consider the longer-term implications of such reliance for the political and economic viability of the French polity. In contrast to the 1960s strategy, French energy policy in the 1970s was characterized by active state intervention in almost all energy-related activities with the express purpose of controlling energy production and consumption patterns rather than allowing the international energy market to create them. Policy in the 1970s was oriented toward the future; it attempted to anticipate the problems that resulted from dependence on a resource increasingly subject to arbitrary manipulations as supplies declined. Finally, policymaking was marked by the increasing salience of comprehensive analysis required to inform such choices.

French public officials, in responding to the energy-related problems that emerged in the 1970s, moved to a considerably more rational-analytic approach than had marked the nation's energy policy during the 1960s.

For the Netherlands, the energy White Paper represented a significant departure from the incremental approach to energy policy that had prevailed throughout the post-war period. Rather than allow the discrete decisions of the mar-

ketplace to determine the country's energy patterns, significant government intervention was foreseen across a broad
range of issues. Moreover, rather than focusing exclusively
on economic and market criteria, the environmental and
social implications of various energy technologies were acknowledged as important in future energy policy choices.
Finally, instead of being preoccupied with immediate energy
concerns (the Netherlands, after all, had just become a net
energy exporter), policy began to give major consideration to
future energy production and consumption patterns in the
Netherlands.

The studies in this book show that it was not by chance
that anti-nuclear forces became national movements to be
reckoned with in the mid-1970s. Although opposition to
nuclear power had existed earlier, it had been a scattered,
localized phenomenon with largely parochial concerns. To
use the incremental argument, the application of a more
comprehensive, rational-analytic strategy to the articulation of energy policy pushed energy-related concerns onto
the national political agenda. Energy policy became highly
politicized, with the focus being primarily, but not exclusively, on nuclear power. Contrary to the other point argued
in the incremental literature, however, this politicization
did not necessarily result in political stalemate, as we have
seen in the varying degrees of success enjoyed by governments in the execution of their energy policies. In other
words, although analysis of overall decision-making strategies helps to explain why nuclear power was pushed to the
top of the political agenda, it is less useful in accounting for
the different outcomes. Here, the structure of the policymaking process itself is critical.

The preceding analysis points to the intimate link between a country's political structure and the policy options
available to its energy officials. The relatively pluralistic
political systems of West Germany and the Netherlands
have allowed diverse groups in both countries to participate
in the policymaking process and, in so doing, to place con-

siderable constraints on the actions of government. In contrast, the French system—highly centralized and dominated by state agencies and their officials—is so structured that access to the policymaking process is quite restricted. The state as a consequence has been relatively unencumbered in pursuit of its favored energy policy objectives.

In conclusion, energy policy is not simply a matter of economic choice, ecological necessity, or geological *fortuna*. Politics is central to the analysis of energy policy. It is not my purpose in this study to propose a set of recommendations for a "better" energy policy. Such an exercise would tend to reflect only my personal values. What I have hoped to show in my analysis is that any reform, regardless of its normative intent, must be based on a sound understanding of the political process.

Nevertheless, the study of energy policy in West Germany, France, and the Netherlands does possess certain normative implications. If the three countries continue along their present courses—France pursuing a thoroughgoing nuclear strategy, West Germany taking a middle road, and the Netherlands shunning the nuclear power option—their experiences may provide a concrete basis upon which to evaluate the nuclear option.

Appendix

Table 1. Primary energy consumption in the FRG, 1950—1975 In mtce (percentage of total)

	1950	1955	1957	1958	1960	1965	1968	1970	1972	1973	1975
Hard coal	98.7 (72.8)	131.3 (71.7)	136.4 (69.8)	124.9 (65.5)	128.4 (60.7)	114.4 (43.2)	98.0 (34.0)	96.8 (28.8)	83.4 (23.6)	84.1 (22.2)	66.5 (19.1)
Soft coal (lignite)	20.7 (15.3)	27.3 (14.9)	29.0 (14.8)	28.8 (15.1)	29.2 (13.8)	30.0 (11.4)	28.7 (9.9)	30.6 (9.1)	31.0 (8.7)	33.1 (8.7)	34.4 (9.9)
Oil	6.3 (4.6)	15.5 (8.5)	21.5 (11.0)	27.8 (14.6)	44.4 (21.0)	108.0 (40.8)	142.4 (49.4)	178.9 (53.1)	196.4 (55.4)	209.0 (55.2)	181.0 (52.1)
Natural gas	—	.4 (.2)	.6 (.3)	.6 (.3)	.8 (.4)	3.5 (1.3)	9.3 (3.2)	18.3 (5.4)	30.6 (8.6)	38.6 (10.2)	48.7 (14.0)
Hydro	6.2 (4.6)	6.1 (3.3)	5.6 (2.9)	6.4 (3.4)	6.6 (3.1)	5.2 (2.0)	5.4 (1.9)	5.7 (1.7)	4.1 (1.2)	4.7 (1.3)	—
Nuclear	—	—	—	—	—	—	.6 (.2)	2.1 (.6)	3.1 (.9)	4.0 (1.1)	7.1 (2.0)
Other	3.6 (2.7)	2.5 (1.4)	2.4 (1.2)	2.1 (1.1)	2.0 (1.0)	3.5 (1.7)	4.1 (1.4)	4.4 (1.3)	5.7 (1.6)	5.0 (3.4)	10.0 (2.9)
Total	135.5	183.2	195.5	190.7	211.5	264.6	288.5	336.8	354.3	378.6	347.7
Net imports (%)	—	—	6.0	12.2	12.2	34.8	42.5	50.0	55.0	56.6	

Sources: Julius Kruse, *Energiewirtschaft* (Berlin: Duncker & Humbolt, 1972), pp. 36–37; *Erste Fortschreibung des Energieprogramms der Bundesregierung* (Bundesministerium fuer Wirtschaft, Nov. 1974), Anhang 1; *Energy Policy Program, Second Revision* (BmWi, 14 Dec. 1977), p. 43; Martin Meyer-Renschhausen, *Energiepolitik in der BRD von 1950 bis heute* (Cologne: Pahl-Regenstein Verlag, 1977), p. 23.

Table 2. Primary energy production in the FRG, 1950–
1972 In mtce (percentage of total)

	1950	1955	1957	1960	1965	1970	1972
Hard coal	126.2 (79.8)	149.1 (79.6)	150.8 (77.9)	143.3 (77.2)	135.5 (77.3)	112.2 (64.4)	103.6 (60.0)
Soft coal (lignite)	20.9 (13.2)	24.8 (13.3)	26.6 (13.9)	26.3 (14.2)	27.7 (15.0)	29.7 (17.1)	29.9 (17.3)
Oil	1.6 (1.0)	4.5 (2.4)	5.0 (2.9)	8.0 (4.3)	11.4 (6.2)	10.8 (6.2)	10.2 (5.9)
Natural gas	0.1 (0.1)	0.6 (0.3)	0.8 (0.4)	1.1 (0.6)	3.6 (1.9)	14.3 (8.2)	20.1 (11.6)
Hydro	5.6 (3.5)	5.5 (2.9)	5.3 (2.8)	4.9 (2.6)	5.2 (2.8)	6.2 (3.6)	7.0 (4.1)
Other	3.6 (2.3)	2.6 (1.4)	2.4 (2.1)	2.0 (1.1)	1.9 (1.0)	1.1 (0.6)	0.9 (0.5)
Total	158.1	187.1	191.5	185.6	185.2	174.1	172.6

Sources: Meyer-Renschhausen, Energiepolitik, p. 20; Kruse, Energiewirtschaft, pp. 36–37.

Table 3. Coal mining in the FRG, 1950–1973

	Pro- duction (mt)	Employ- ment (1000)	Productiv- ity (kg/man)	Stock- piles (mt)	Total sales (mt)	Exported sales (mt)
1950	126.2	536.8	1405	—	—	—
1957	150.8	604.0	1599	1.0	—	—
1959	142.6	—	—	17.8	—	—
1961	142.7	465.0	2207	11.7	117	28
1963	142.1	412.0	2521	3.8	126	30
1965	135.1	377.0	2705	15.4	106	24
1966	126.0	334.0	2926	20.4	98	25
1968	112.0	264.0	3526	9.5	103	30
1970	111.3	253.0	3755	1.2	113	26
1973	97.3	205.0	4068	14.9	98	24

Sources: Erste Fortschreibung, Anhang 5; Kruse, Energiewirtschaft, pp.
106, 111; Meyer-Renschhausen, Energiepolitik, p. 161.

Table 4. Coal and oil prices (DM per ton) in the FRG, 1957–1966

	German Coal at Pit Head	Freight Rates U.S.-North Sea	U.S. Coal (cif) North Sea	1000 CE Fuel Oil
1957	63.29	29.20	76.50	95.20
1958	64.53	13.30	58.20	80.22
1960	62.70	15.10	58.40	54.74
1963	63.87	15.50	58.90	42.25
1966	67.00	12.70	58.80	37.36

Source: Meyer-Renschhausen, Energiepolitik, p. 51.

Table 5. French energy consumption, 1954–1974 In mtce

	1954	1960	1964	1970	1973	1974
Coal						
Production	56.3	58.3	55.8	40.6	29.1	26.8
Imports	10.9	12.0	18.5	16.6	16.6	20.1
Petroleum						
Production	0.6	2.8	4.0	3.2	1.8	1.5
Imports	24.8	37.5	63.0	127.8	172.7	165.9
Natural gas						
Production	0.4	4.5	7.6	10.0	10.6	10.6
Imports	0.0	0.0	0.0	3.9	11.8	13.5
Primary electricity						
Production	8.0	13.4	12.5	20.4	19.4	23.3
Total production	65.3	79.0	79.9	74.2	60.9	62.2
Net imports	35.7	49.4	81.5	148.3	201.2	199.5
Covered by national resources %	64.6	62.0	49.1	33.4	23.6	23.8

Source: EDF compilation of data from French Committee for World Energy Conference and Commission de l'energie du plan (Paris: La Documentation Francaise, 1975); reprinted from Dominique Saumon and Louis Puiseux, "Actors and Decisions in French Energy Policy," in The Energy Syndrome, ed. Leon N. Lindberg (Lexington, Mass.: Lexington Books, 1977).

Table 6. Economic performance of advanced industrial democracies

	1972	1973	1974	1975	1976	1977	1978	1979	1980
GDP growth (%)									
United States	5.5	5.4	-0.6	-0.9	5.4	5.4	4.4	2.8	-0.2
Japan	8.8	8.8	-1.0	2.3	5.3	5.3	5.0	5.5	4.2
West Germany	3.7	4.9	0.5	-1.8	5.2	3.0	3.3	4.6	1.8
France	5.9	5.4	3.2	0.2	5.2	3.1	3.7	3.5	1.3
Great Britain	2.2	7.5	-1.2	-0.6	3.6	1.3	3.3	1.4	-1.8
Italy	3.2	7.0	4.1	-3.6	5.9	1.9	2.7	4.9	4.0
Inflation (%)									
United States	2.3	6.2	11.0	9.1	5.8	6.5	7.7	11.3	13.5
Japan	4.5	11.7	24.5	11.8	9.3	8.1	3.8	3.6	8.0
West Germany	5.5	6.9	7.0	6.0	4.5	3.7	2.7	4.1	5.5
France	6.2	7.3	13.7	11.8	9.6	9.4	9.1	10.8	13.6
Great Britain	7.1	9.2	16.0	24.2	16.5	15.8	8.3	13.4	18.0
Italy	5.7	10.8	19.1	17.0	16.8	18.4	12.1	14.8	21.2
Unemployment (%)									
United States	5.4	4.7	5.4	8.3	7.5	6.9	5.9	5.7	7.0
Japan	1.4	1.3	1.4	1.9	2.0	2.0	2.2	2.1	2.0
West Germany	0.8	0.9	1.6	3.7	3.7	3.7	3.5	3.2	3.1
France	2.7	2.6	2.8	4.1	4.4	4.7	5.2	5.9	6.3
Great Britain	4.1	3.0	2.9	3.9	5.5	6.2	6.1	5.7	7.4
Italy	6.3	6.2	5.3	5.8	6.6	7.0	7.1	7.5	7.4
Bal. of payments (billion $)									
United States	-9.9	-0.4	-5.0	18.3	4.6	-14.1	-13.9	1.4	3.7
Japan	6.6	-0.1	-4.7	-0.7	3.7	10.9	16.5	-8.8	-10.7
West Germany	0.8	4.3	9.7	3.5	3.4	4.2	8.7	-6.2	-16.5
France	0.3	-0.7	-6.0	-0.1	-6.1	-3.3	4.1	1.2	-7.8
Great Britain	0.4	-1.8	-7.9	-3.6	-1.5	0.5	2.0	-3.7	7.4
Italy	2.3	-2.5	-8.0	-0.6	-2.9	2.3	6.3	5.5	-9.7
Petroleum imports (tbd)									
United States		6256		6056	7295	8808	8228	6519	5220
Japan		5576		5008	5235	5454	5347	4846	4373
West Germany		3046		2509	2809	2768	2848	2147	1953
France		2875		2278	2598	2514	2494	2520	2182
Great Britain		2738		2067	2052	1691	1596	1157	893
Italy		2669		2121	2268	2302	2363	2292	1860

Sources: Daniel Yergin and Martin Hillenbrand, eds., *Global Insecurity* (Boston: Houghton Mifflin, 1982), appendix; U.S. Central Intelligence Agency, Directorate of Intelligence, *Economic and Energy Indicators* (21 Jan. 1983); U.S. Department of Commerce, *International Economic Indicators* (Nov. 1975, March 1978, Dec. 1979).

Table 7. First FRG energy program, 1973

	1972		1975		1980		1985	
	mtce	% of total	mtce	% of total	mtce	% of total	mtce	% of total
Oil	196.4	55.4	230	57	275	54	330	54
Coal	83.7	23.6	72	18	58	11	50	8
Natural gas	30.6	8.6	48	12	82	16	92	15
Lignite	31.0	8.7	35	8	39	8	38	6
Nuclear	3.1	0.9	12	3	45	9	90	15
Other	9.6	2.8	9	2	11	2	10	2
Total	354.3	100.0	406	100	510	100	610	100

Source: *Die Energiepolitik der Bundesregierung* (Bundesrat, Drucksache 607/73, 3 Oct. 1973).

Table 8. First revision of FRG energy program, 1974

	1973		1980		1985	
	mtce	% of total	mtce	% of total	mtce	% of total
Oil	209.0	55	221	47	245	44
Hard coal	84.2	22	82	17	79	14
Natural gas	38.6	10	87	18	101	18
Lignite	33.1	9	35	7	38	7
Nuclear	4.0	1	40	9	81	15
Other	9.7	3	10	2	11	2
Total	378.6	100	475	100	555	100

Source: Erste Fortschreibung.

Table 9. French energy program, 1975

| | 1973 | | 1985 | |
	mtpe	% of total	mtpe	% of total
Oil	116	66	96	40
Coal	30	17	30	13
Gas	15	9	37	15.5
Nuclear	3	2	60	25
Hydro	11	6	14	5.5
New energies	0	0	3	1
Total	175	100	240	100

Source: Ministère de l'Industrie et de la Recherche, *Conseil Central de Planification* (Paris, 3 Feb. 1975).

Table 10. Gas revenues in the Netherlands

	Revenue (Fl mn)	Sales Abroad	Share in Total Revenue (%)	Share in National Income (%)
1974	2,368	911	4.4	1.4
1978	8,642	3,956	9.9	3.4
1979	8,457	3,679	8.8	3.1
1980[a]	12,061	5,568	11.3	4.2
1981[a]	16,745	8,227	14.5	5.5

Source: The Economist Intelligence Unit, *Quarterly Economic Review of the Netherlands* (Fourth Quarter, 1980).
[a]Estimated.

Table 11. Election results in the FRG (percentage)

	CDU/CSU	SPD	FDP	Greens
Hamburg				
1974	40.6	44.9	10.9	
June 1978	37.6	51.5	4.8	4.5
June 1982	43.2	42.8	4.8	7.7
December 1982	38.3	51.3	2.6	6.8
Lower Saxony				
1975	48.8	43.1	7.0	
June 1979	48.7	42.2	4.2	3.9
March 1982	50.7	36.5	5.9	6.5
Hesse				
1974	47.3	43.2	7.4	
October 1978	59.6	31.3	6.0	1.7
September 1982	45.6	42.8	3.1	8.0
September 1983	39.4	46.2	7.6	5.9
Bavaria				
1974	62.1	30.2	5.2	
October 1978	59.6	31.3	6.0	1.7
October 1982	58.3	31.9	3.5	4.6
Berlin				
1975	43.9	42.6	7.1	
March 1979	44.4	42.6	8.1	3.7
May 1981	47.9	38.4	5.6	7.3
Rhineland-Palatinate				
1975	53.9	38.5	5.6	
March 1979	50.1	42.3	6.4	
Schleswig-Holstein				
1975	50.4	40.1	7.1	
April 1979	48.3	41.7	5.8	2.4
Bremen				
1975	33.9	48.8	13.0	
October 1979	31.9	49.4	10.7	5.1
September 1983	33.3	51.4	4.6	5.4
Baden-Wuerttemberg				
1976	56.7	33.3	7.8	
March 1980	53.4	32.5	8.3	5.3
March 1984	51.9	32.4	7.2	8.0
Saarland				
1976	49.1	41.8	7.4	
April 1980	44.0	45.4	6.9	2.9
North Rhine-Westphalia				
1976	47.0	45.0	7.8	
May 1980	43.2	48.4	4.986	3.0
Bundestag				
October 1980	44.5	42.9	10.6	1.5
March 1983	48.8	38.2	6.9	5.6

Table 12. Attitudes toward nuclear power in West Germany and France

West Germany			

Question: Do nuclear power plants represent a threat to the safety of the population, or is there no reason to be concerned about safety problems?

	A threat	No threat	No opinion
Total population (1,196)	41%	37%	22%
Sex			
Men	41%	42%	17%
Women	42%	33%	25%
Age			
18–24 years	55%	28%	17%
25–34 years	44%	40%	16%
35–49 years	37%	43%	20%
50–64 years	41%	38%	21%
65 years and above	37%	32%	31%
Occupation			
Farmers	28%	72%	0%
Professionals	19%	51%	30%
Civil service, employees,			
(white collar)	40%	42%	18%
Skilled blue collar	42%	45%	13%
Unskilled blue collar	56%	29%	15%
Education			
Primary	43%	32%	25%
Primary and apprenticeship	39%	39%	22%
Primary and professional	41%	42%	17%
High school and university	47%	37%	16%
Production unit			
–100	41%	36%	23%
101–2000	44%	38%	18%
2000 +	35%	47%	18%
Union affiliation			
Labor union members	40%	43%	17%
Nonunion members	42%	36%	22%
Religion			
Catholic	37%	37%	26%
Protestant	44%	38%	18%
None or other	54%	35%	11%

Source: Poll INFAS, May 1977

Table 12, continued

France

Question: Are you for or against the development of nuclear power plants?

	Against	For	No opinion
Total	42%	47%	11%
Sex			
Men	39%	54%	7%
Women	46%	42%	12%
Age			
18–24 years	54%	38%	8%
25–34 years	55%	38%	7%
35–49 years	37%	49%	14%
50–64 years	33%	55%	12%
65 years and above	37%	54%	9%
Occupation			
Farmers	42%	41%	17%
Small business	44%	43%	13%
Professionals and big business	29%	64%	7%
White collar	44%	49%	7%
Blue collar	48%	39%	13%
Retired, nonworking	40%	53%	7%
Education[a]			
Primary	33.5%	51.0%	15.5%
Primary-superior	32.0%	62.0%	6.0%
Secondary	33.0%	62.0%	5.0%
Technical-commercial	30.0%	63.0%	7.0%
Higher education	40.0%	55.5%	4.5%

Source: SOFRES; reported in Figaro, Dec. 1978.

[a]This item is from 1976 survey, asking the same question (SOFRES, 1976; reported in F. Fagnani and A. Nicolon, eds., Nucléopolis: Matériaux pour l'analyse d'une société nucléaire [Grenoble: PUG, 1979]).

Both surveys are reprinted from Dorothy Nelkin and Michael Pollak, The Atom Besieged (Cambridge, Mass.: MIT Press, 1981), pp. 110, 112.

Notes

1. ENERGY POLICIES AND NATIONAL AGENDAS

1. See, for example, Robert L. Heilbroner, *An Inquiry into the Human Prospect* (New York: W. W. Norton, 1974); Mihajlo Mesarovic and Eduard Pestel, *Mankind at the Turning Point* (New York: Signet, 1974).

2. Leon N. Lindberg, *The Energy Syndrome* (Lexington, Mass.: D.C. Heath, 1977), pp. 4, 336.

3. See Todd R. LaPorte, "Organized Social Complexity: Explication of a Concept," in *Organized Social Complexity: Challenge to Politics and Policy*, ed. LaPorte (Princeton, N.J.: Princeton Univ. Press, 1975), pp. 3-21; and Ernst B. Haas, "Is there a hole in the whole? Knowledge, technology, interdependence, and the construction of international regimes," *International Organization* 29 (Summer 1975): 827-76.

4. This same tendency toward demands for greater comprehensiveness has been noted in various energy studies on the United States as well. See, for example, Don E. Kash and Robert Rycroft, *U.S. Energy Policy: Crisis and Complacency* (Norman: Univ. of Oklahoma Press, 1984); David Howard Davis, *Energy Politics*, 3d ed. (New York: St. Martin's Press, 1982); Charles O. Jones, "American Politics and the Organization of Energy Decision Making," *Annual Review of Energy* 4 (1979): 99-121.

2. WORLD ENERGY MARKETS AND NATIONAL POLICY

1. For details of these and complementary arrangements, see John M. Blair, *The Control of Oil* (New York: Vintage Books, 1978), chs. 2, 3.

2. For a detailed discussion of the circumstances behind the transition from cartel to oligopoly, see Peter F. Cowhey, *The Problems of Plenty: Energy Policy and International Politics* (Berkeley: Univ. of California Press, 1985), ch. 4.

3. Ibid., pp. 4-5.

4. Although the coal crisis resulted largely from increased competitiveness of oil, other factors also contributed. Important was the halving transatlantic freight rates in 1958, which made coal mined in the United States much more competitive on the West German market. See M.A.

Adelman, *The World Petroleum Market* (Baltimore, Md.: Johns Hopkins Univ. Press, 1973), p. 269.

5. Whereas the consumption of hard coal (lignite) declined from 80.6% (15.1%) of total energy consumption in 1958 to 28.7% (9.1%) in 1970, the proportion of hard coal (lignite) used in public power plants went from just 52.5% (45.8%) to 37.9% (42.2%) during this same period (see Tables 1 and 3). That is, the substitution process was much slower in the power generating sector than the other areas of energy consumption. Further, government expenditures on Ruhr coal mining had tripled over an eight-year period: from DM 855.1 million in 1958, subsidies had risen to DM 2.508 billion in 1966. Martin Meyer-Renschhausen, *Energiepolitik in der BRD von 1950 bis heute* (Koeln: Pahl-Rugenstein Verlag, 1977), p. 85.

6. For a more detailed discussion of the factors determining the failures or successes of the various strategies, see Michael T. Hatch, "The Management of Postindustrial Problems in Western Europe: Energy Policy in the Federal Republic of Germany, France, and the Netherlands" Ph.D. diss., Univ. of California, Berkeley, 1983, ch. 2.

7. See Stanley Hoffmann, "The Paradoxes of the French Political Community," in *In Search of France*, by Stanley Hoffmann and others (New York: Harper and Row, 1963).

8. Stephen S. Cohen, *Modern Capitalist Planning: The French Model* (Berkeley: Univ. of California Press, 1977).

9. In March 1928, an oil law was passed which stipulated that the government was to authorize the import of petroleum products, giving special preference to crude oil imports over finished products. In 1931, on the basis of this statute, the refining affiliate of Compagnie Française des Pétroles (CFP), a French oil company founded at the initiative and partially owned by the French government, was given 58.4% of the domestic market, with the French affiliates of the international majors allotted 41.6%. Following the Second World War, application of the 1928 law was suspended through 1950. The 1951 arrangement was somewhat more favorable to the international affiliates—49.6% for the French group, 50.4% for the foreign companies.

10. Michel Vilain, *La Politique de l'Energie en France* (Paris: Editions Cujas, 1969), pp. 122-32, 142; Peter A. Odell, *Oil and World Power: Background to the Oil Crisis* (New York: Taplinger Publishing, 1975), p. 204.

11. Cohen, *Modern Capitalist Planning*, pp. 142-43.

12. Energy demand during the Third Plan: 1957, 122.7 mtce; 1958, 121 mtce; 1959, 122.6 mtce; 1960, 125.8 mtce; 1961, 137 mtce. Vilain, *La Politique de L'Energie*, p. 44.

13. Ibid., p. 117.

14. In addition to increased natural gas production from a recently discoverd natural gas field at Lacq, the Third Plan called for all increases in oil consumption to be met by oil production in the franc zone. Cohen, *Modern Capitalist Planning*, p. 284.

15. Coal production during the period: 1957, 57.9 mt; 1962, 53.7 mt; 1967, 49.3 mt; 1970, 38.9 mt. In 1968, after continual downward revisions, the government announced its intention to reduce output to 25 mt by 1975, despite efforts to slow the decline. For a more detailed discussion of the problems of the coal sector, see Michel Toromanoff, *Le drame des houilleres* (Paris: Editions du Seuil, 1969); Dominique Saumon and Louis Puiseux, "Actors and Decisions in French Energy Policy," in *The Energy Syndrome*, pp. 127-28, 138-41.

16. French oil companies were to pay $2.08 per barrel, as opposed to $1.80 posted world price and $2.35 for foreign companies. Higher energy costs for French industry that resulted from differences in the price of Algerian crude as opposed to crude purchased on the world market were largely offset by very low taxes on fuel oil, when compared to West Germany and Great Britain; however, because of the price differential between Algerian crude and oil purchased on the international market, a *devoir national* (national obligation) was established that required refiners in France to buy certain quantities of the more expensive Algerian oil (at least 55% of their production for the domestic market) from French crude producers as a condition for continued authorization to import and operate in France. See Michel Grenon, *Pour une Politique de l'Energie* (Paris: Marabout Université, 1972), p. 26; and Horst Mendershausen, *Coping with the Oil Crisis* (Baltimore, Md.: Johns Hopkins Univ. Press, 1976), p. 26.

17. From Philippe Simonnot, *Les Nucléocrates* (Grenoble: Presses Universitaires de Grenoble, 1978.), p. 248. For a more detailed discussion of planning within the context of French energy policy, see Hatch, "Management of Postindustrial Problems," ch. 4; for a somewhat different approach to this issue, as well as a detailed analysis of French energy policy itself, see N.J.D. Lucas, *Energy in France: Planning, Politics, and Policy* (London: Europa Publications, 1979).

18. Rates in GDP growth in other countries in 1950-60 (1960-65): West Germany, 7.9% (4.9%), UK, 2.8% (3.3%), Belgium, 3.1% (4.9%), US, 3.3% (4.7%). See James Goodear Abert, *Economic Policy and Planning in the Netherlands, 1950-65* (New Haven, Conn.: Yale Univ. Press, 1969), pp. 7-9.

19. By 1952, domestic coal production of approximately 12.5 mt approached the 1938 level of 13.5 mt; in energy dependence, the ratio of domestic energy production—coal plus small quantities of oil and natural gas—to total consumption declined throughout the 1950s: 1950, 65%; 1953, 60%; 1955, 52%; 1957, 48%.

20. See Abert, *Economic Policy in the Netherlands*, p. 1.

21. Nevertheless, by the early 1960s, efforts to keep wage increases below rises in productivity were proving unsuccessful. The Netherlands had experienced several years of full employment, and increasing numbers of Dutch workers were finding employment on the German side of the border where wages were considerably higher. Under these conditions, incomes

policy was becoming less effective at keeping costs and prices at levels that would maintain a strong competitive position for Dutch exports. See Andrew Shonfield, *Modern Capitalism* (London: Oxford Univ. Press, 1965), p. 213.

22. J.E. Hartshorn, *Politics and World Oil Economics* (New York: Praeger, 1967), p. 261.

23. While ultimate authority in pricing policy resided with the Dutch government, which controlled transfer prices and approved tariffs, the government largely acquiesced to the private companies.

24. Joel Darmstadter, *Energy in the World Economy* (Baltimore, Md.: Johns Hopkins Univ. Press, 1971), p. 656; "Le Gaz Naturel dans l'Economie Nederlandaise," *Problemes Economiques*, 21 Dec. 1977, p. 26.

25. Cowhey, *Problems of Plenty*, ch. 5, p. 2. Even more telling were the projected estimates of U.S. imports if this trend continued: by 1985 the United States would be importing from 50 to 60% of its total oil supply, 30 to 40% of which would be from the Eastern Hemisphere. See "Official Background Summary and Fact Sheet" issued by the Office of the White House Press Secretary; and Ruth Sheldon Knowles, *America's Oil Famine* (New York: Coward, McCann and Geoghegan, 1975), p. 11.

26. Revenue stability was managed primarily through an agreement with the majors that changed the tax base from actual prices, which had been declining, to stable posted prices. See Blair, *Control of Oil*, p. 261.

27. For a more detailed discussion of the negotiations surrounding the Libyan, Tehran, and Tripoli agreements, especially why the oil companies didn't seem to resist the changes as strongly as expected, see Cowhey, *Problems of Plenty*, ch. 5; Blair, *Control of Oil*, ch. 9; Benjamin Schwadran, *Middle East Oil* (Cambridge, Mass.: Shenkman Publishing, 1977), pp. 12-21.

28. Schwadran, *Middle East Oil*, pp. 63-65.

29. The largest majors were Esso with 20% of German refining capacity, Shell with 13%, and BP with 12%; the largest German companies were Gelsenberg (6%) and Oberrheinische Mineraloelwerke (6%). Julius Kruse, *Energiewirtschaft* (Berlin: Duncker & Humbolt, 1972), pp. 153-56.

30. Vilain, *La Politique de L'Energie*, pp. 322-23.

31. W.G. Jensen, *Energy in Europe: 1945-1980* (London: G.T. Foulis, 1967), pp. 141-42. See also *Petroleum Press Service*, Feb. 1969, pp. 49-50, and ibid., March 1969, p. 105.

32. Mendershausen, *Coping with the Oil Crisis*, p. 29.

33. Saumon and Puiseux, "Actors and Decisions," pp. 126-27.

34. Blair, *Control of Oil*, p. 264.

35. OPEC's production in early 1975 was approximately 34 mbd (with production capacity put at 38 mbd); world demand for the first quarter of 1975, on the other hand, averaged 26.5 mbd. Dankwart A. Rostow and John F. Mugno, *OPEC: Success and Prospects* (New York: Council on Foreign Relations Books, 1976), p. 31.

36. See, for example, Rostow and Mugno, ibid., pp. 46-47; Anthony Sampson, *The Seven Sisters* (New York: Bantam, 1976), pp. 359-60.

37. Cowhey, *Problems of Plenty*, ch. 6, pp. 5, 13-14.

38. Daniel Yergin and Martin Hillenbrand, eds., *Global Insecurity* (New York: Penguin, 1983), p. 324.

39. Before the crisis, Iranian production had averaged between 5.3 and 6 mbd. During January and February 1979, virtually all production ceased. It resumed in subsequent months but at a lower level. To compensate partially for lost Iranian production, Saudi Arabia and several other OPEC members increased their output by approximately 1 mbd. See Yergin and Hillenbrand, *Global Insecurity*, p. 325; Cowhey, *Problems of Plenty*, ch. 6, p. 6.

40. Cowhey, *Problems of Plenty*, pp. 6, 9.

41. See *The Economist*, 20 Nov. 1982, p. 74.

42. The high absorbers of OPEC—Nigeria, Indonesia, Venezuela, Algeria, Iraq, Iran, Ecuador, and Gabon—ran a collective current-accounts deficit of $23-25 billion in 1982. *The Economist*, 10 Dec. 1983, p. 68.

3. THE ENERGY CRISES OF THE 1970s

1. *Erste Fortschreibung des Energieprogramms der Bundesregierung* (Bundesministerium fuer Wirtschaft, Nov. 1974), p. 8.

2. Ibid., p. 10.

3. Ibid., pp. 8-9.

4. See Mendershausen, *Coping with the Oil Crisis*, pp. 75-78; and *OECD Economic Surveys—Germany* (Paris: OECD, July 1975).

5. *Erste Fortschreibung*, pp. 12-13; and Mendershausen, *Coping with the Oil Crisis*, p. 92.

6. See Mendershausen, *Coping with the Oil Crisis*, pp. 78-79.

7. Ibid., pp. 68-71.

8. *Erste Fortschreibung*, p. 6.

9. For details, see the Bundesrat document containing the energy program: *Die Energiepolitik der Bundesregierung*, (Bundesrat, Drucksache 607/73, 3 Oct. 1973).

10. *Erste Fortschreibung*, pp. 30-50.

11. See *Der Spiegel*, 12 Dec. 1977; and *Energy Policy Programme for the Federal Republic of Germany: Second Revision* (Bundesministerium fuer Wirtschaft, 14 Dec. 1977).

12. Dieter Schmitt, "West German Energy Policy," in *After the Second Oil Crisis*, ed. Wilfrid L. Kohl (Lexington, Mass.: Lexington Books, 1982), p. 146.

13. See *Die Zeit*, 16 April 1976.

14. *Petroleum Economist*, April 1982.

15. *Sueddeutsche Zeitung*, 21 May 1975.

16. See *Die Zeit*, 21 Nov. 1975.

17. In 1980, petroleum sales declined 11.4% and in the first half of 1981, sales dropped a further 19%. *Die Zeit,* 24 and 31 July 1981. There was a DM 50 per ton loss on petroleum products that totaled approximately DM 5.5 b. *Petroleum Economist,* May 1982, p. 199.

18. Specifically, the agreement called for the sale of a portion of Veba's refining capacity, approximately 1,000 service stations, and 25% participation in Ruhrgas to BP. In return, Veba was to receive DM 800 million and 3 million tons of crude oil per year up to the year 2000.

19. The role of public education was given high priority, the federal/ Laender program was continued, investments for conservation measures in public buildings and transportation were proposed, and considerable emphasis was placed on the expanded use of cogeneration—in December 1981, DM 1.2 billion were committed by federal and Laender governments for district heating over the next five years. For further details, see *Energy Policies and Programmes of the IEA Countries: 1981 Review* (Paris: IEA, 1982), pp. 172-75; and Klaus-Michael Meyer-Abich, "Energy Issues and Policies in the Federal Republic of Germany," in *Annual Review of Energy* 7 (1982): 238-39.

20. Hans-Wilhelm Schiffer, "Entwicklung and struktureller Wandel im Energieverbrauch der Bundesrepublik Deutschland seit 1979," *Zeitschrift fuer Energiewirtschaft* 3 (1983); cited in *Petroleum Economist,* Dec. 1983.

21. For details, see André L. Giraud, "Energy in France," *Annual Review of Energy* 8 (1983): 167-73.

22. Elf-Aquitane was the product of a merger in 1976 between Elf-ERAP and the Société Nationale des Pétroles d'Aquitaine undertaken at the urging of the French government; the state holds a 70% interest in the company.

23. For a critical analysis of French oil policy in general, see Harry B. Feigenbaum, "France's oil policy: the limits of mercantilism," in *France in the Troubled World Economy,* ed. Stephen S. Cohen and Peter A. Gourevitch, (London: Butterworth, 1982).

24. See Geraud, "Energy in France," pp. 179, 189-90.

25. *The Economist,* 3 Sept. 1983, p. 62; *Petroleum Economist,* May 1984.

26. Guy de Carmoy, "French Energy Policy," in *After the Second Oil Crisis,* ed. Wilfrid L. Kohl (Lexington, Mass.: Lexington Books, 1982), p. 132.

27. *Energy Use and Planning in France* (French Embassy, Press and Information, Doc. 83/22), pp. 6-7.

28. *Summary of the Paper on the Energy Policy,* Ministry of Economic Affairs, p. 2.

29. See Philip B. Smith and Ruud Spanhoff, "The Nuclear Energy Debate in the Netherlands," *Bulletin of the Atomic Scientists* (Feb. 1976), pp. 41-44.

30. *Petroleum Economist,* Sept. 1983.

31. See *Petroleum Economist,* Oct. 1980, p. 448.

32. *Petroleum Economist*, Dec. 1983, pp. 463-64.

33. See *The Economist*, 11 Oct. 1980; *Petroleum Economist*, April 1980.

34. See *Energy Conservation in the International Energy Agency: 1978 Review* (OECD, Paris, 1979); *News Bulletin* (the Hague), 2 July, 3 Aug. 1978.

35. For further details on conservation, see *Energy Policy and Programmes of the IEA Countries, 1981 Review* (Paris: IEA), pp. 241-43.

36. *IEA Review, 1981*, p. 241.

37. Although other factors, such as recent economic recession, affected energy use, conservation surely had something to do with the drop in total energy consumption in 1982, when use (44.1 mtoe) was 12% below the 1973 level (50.2 mtoe). *The Economist*, 11 Feb. 1984, p. 69.

4. UNRAVELING CONSENSUS IN WEST GERMANY

1. For a discussion of German nuclear R&D policy in the 1950s and 1960s, see Henry R. Nau, *National Politics and International Technology* (Baltimore, Md.: Johns Hopkins Univ. Press, 1974), pp. 72-76, 85-87, 91-93.

2. See *Einstellung und Verhalten der Bevoelkerung gegenueber verschiedenen Energiegewinnungsarten*, Battel Institut, June 1977.

3. For a more detailed description of these events from the perspective of the anti-nuclear groups, see Hans-Helmut Wuestenhagen, *Buerger gegen Kernkraftwerke*, (Hamburg: rororo, 1975).

4. For a more detailed account of these events and the German antinuclear movement in general, see Dorothy Nelkin and Michael Pollak, *The Atom Besieged: Extraparliamentary Dissent in France and West Germany* (Cambridge: MIT Press, 1981).

5. See Wuestenhagen, *Buerger gegen Kernkraftwerke*.

6. *Wirtschaftswoche*, 8 April 1977.

7. Hans Matthoefer, "Bewaehrungsprobe fuer die Demokratie," *Umwelt*, May 1975, p. 4.

8. *Vorwaerts*, 28 Aug. 1975.

9. Hans Matthoefer, "Kernenergie—Die Bewaeltigung unserer Zukunft als Chance und Risiko," *Gewerkschaftliche Monatshefte*, Oct. 1977, p. 633.

10. "Die Frage heisst: Wie wollen kuenftig leben?" a discussion between Hans Matthoefer and Carl Amory on 18 November 1976, sponsored and moderated by *Vorwaerts* (Bonn-Bad Godesberg: Neuer Vorwaerts-Verlag).

11. Hans Matthoefer, *Interviews und Gespraeche zur Kernenergie* (Karlsruhe: C.F. Mueller, 1977), p. 15.

12. *Die Zeit*, 1 April 1977.

13. This ruling was based on an interpretation of Paragraph 7 of the Nuclear Energy Act which requires the most recent scientific and technological advances (*Stand der Wissenschaft und der Technik*) in the area of reactor safety. The concept of an additional containment wall had been

developed for a nuclear reactor that was to be constructed in the heavily-populated area of Ludwigshafen. The project was subsequently abandoned, purportedly because of high costs of the wall, which added an estimated 10% to the cost of the reactor. Critics of the ruling argued that an extra containment wall was a supplemental safety precaution appropriate only to the Ludwigshafen plant because of the population density. As the area surrounding Wyhl was sparsely populated, the wall was unneeded for safety. *Handelsblatt*, 18 March 1977.

14. *Frankfurter Rundschau*, 21 July 1977.

15. See Nau, *National Politics and International Technology*, pp. 87, 151.

16. *Handelsblatt*, 18 March 1977; *Die Zeit*, 27 May 1977; *Die Welt*, 6 Aug. 1977.

17. *Koelner Stadt-Anzeiger*, 31 Aug. 1977.

18. *Frankfurter Rundschau*, 27 March 1977.

19. "Kernenergie und Umweltschuetz," *Stellungnahme des DGB-Bundesvorstandes vom 5. April 1977*.

20. Ibid.

21. "Auszug aus der Regierungserklaerung des Bundeskanzlers vom 16. Dezember 1976," *Forum SPD Energie: Ein Diskussionsleitfaden*, 1977, p. 101.

22. "Grundlinien und Eckwerte fuer die Fortschreibung des Energieprogramms," *Bulletin* 30 (25 March 1977): 278.

23. See *Forum SPD: Fachtagung "Energie, Beschaeftigung, Lebensqualitaet" am 28. und 29. April 1977 in Koeln*: Helmut Schmidt, pp. 156-67, Adolph Schmidt, pp. 31-44, Erhard Eppler, pp. 16-30.

24. "Beschluss zur Energiepolitik," *Bundeshauptausschuss der F.D.P. in Saarbruecken am 26. 6. 1977*, p. 7.

25. See *Der Spiegel*, 26 Sept. 1977.

26. Joerg Hallerbach, ed., *Die Eigentliche Kernspaltung* (Darmstadt: Luchterhand, 1978), pp. 214-15.

27. Ibid., p. 214.

28. For the effects of the union effort, see *Handelsblatt*, 26 Oct. 1977; *Sueddeutsche Zeitung*, 16 Nov. 1977.

29. *Konsequenzen des vom F.D.P.-Hauptausschuss geforderten Kernenergie-Moratorium* (Bonn: Deutsches Atomforum, August 1977).

30. *Beschluss zur Energiepolitik des ordentlichen Bundesparteitags der F.D.P. in Kiel vom 6. bis 8. November 1977*, pp. 5-6.

31. *Beschluesse zur Energiepolitik: SPD Parteitag Hamburg, 15-19 November 1977*, pp. 3, 8.

32. "Grundlinien und Eckwerte," p. 266.

33. See *Energy Programme for the Federal Republic of Germany: Second Revision* (Bundesministerium fuer Wirtschaft, 14 Dec. 1977).

34. Ibid., p. 26.

35. Ibid., pp. 28-29.

5. STALEMATE IN WEST GERMANY

1. See *The Economist*, 16 June 1984, pp. 40-42; *Relay from Bonn*, 30 Nov. 1984. For a more detailed, somewhat sympathetic treatment of the Greens, see Fritjof Capra and Charlene Spretnak, *Green Politics* (New York: E.P. Dutton, 1984).

2. According to demographic studies, although the Green supporters have come from all parties, a larger proportion have been drawn from the SPD and FDP than from the CDU/CSU. In addition, the studies show that potential Green voters are especially numerous in the younger age groups (18-34), in recent years a reservoir from which the SPD drew an overproportional number of supporters. See the *Sueddeutsche Zeitung*, 1, 2 Dec. 1979; *Der Spiegel*, 12 Nov. 1979 and 24 March 1980.

3. See *Sueddeutsche Zeitung*, 15 Dec. 1977; *Stuttgarter Nachrichten*, 5 Oct. 1977; *Der Spiegel*, 3 Oct. 1977.

4. *Wall Street Journal*, 17 May 1979.

5. See *Bericht des Bundesministeriums fuer Forschung und Technologie ueber die Entwicklung des Natriumgekuehlten Schnellbrutreaktors*, 1 Sept. 1977, p. 30.

6. *Relay from Bonn*, 22 Dec. 1978.

7. Karl Kaiser, "The Great Nuclear Debate," *Foreign Policy* 30 (Spring 1978): 90.

8. See Gene I. Rochlin, *Plutonium, Power, and Politics* (Berkeley: Univ. of California Press, 1979), p. 162.

9. Ibid., p. 165.

10. Ibid., pp. 165-66.

11. Ibid., pp. 166-67.

12. For detailed accounts of the German-Brazilian deal and the conflicts it subsequently precipitated between West Germany and the United States, see Kaiser, "Great Nuclear Debate," pp. 83-110; William W. Lowrance, "Nuclear Futures for Sale: To Brazil from West Germany, 1975," *International Security* 1 (Fall 1976): 147-66; Edward Wonder, "Nuclear Commerce and Nuclear Proliferation: Germany and Brazil, 1975," *Orbis* 21 (Summer 1977): 277-306.

13. See Wonder, "Nuclear Commerce," p. 293.

14. Kaiser, "Great Nuclear Debate," p. 89.

15. German officials denied that U.S. pressures had made the safeguards contained in the agreement any stronger. Wonder, "Nuclear Commerce," p. 290.

16. *New York Times*, 13 June 1975.

17. Wonder, "Nuclear Commerce," p. 290.

18. Kaiser, "Great Nuclear Debate," p. 97.

19. Ibid., p. 98.

20. Ibid., p. 99.

21. See *Bericht des BMFT*, pp. 71, 110.

22. *Der Spiegel*, 26 June 1978.

23. For a statement of the intellectual antecedents of Carter's nuclear energy policy, see *Nuclear Power: Issues and Choices* (Cambridge, Mass.: Ballinger, 1977).

24. *Bericht des BMFT*, pp. 43-87, 93-94.

25. Ibid., pp. 93-94.

26. Ibid., pp. 70-71.

27. Ibid., pp. 88-90.

28. *Frankfurter Allgemeine*, 14 May 1977.

29. For a discussion of INFCE from a Carter administration and European perspectives, see the articles by Nye and Lellouche in *International Organization* 35 (Winter 1981).

30. *Die Zeit*, 2 Oct. 1981; *Der Spiegel*, 14 Sept. 1981.

31. For figures, see Meyer-Abich, "Energy Issues and Politics," pp. 244-45.

6. NUCLEAR POWER AND THE FRENCH STATE

1. Saumon and Puiseux, "Actors and Decisions," p. 150.

2. *Atomwirtschaft*, June 1980, p. 282.

3. For an analysis of French nuclear policy and the CEA in the 1940s and 1950s, see Lawrence Scheinman, *Atomic Energy in France under the Fourth Republic* (Princeton, N.J.: Princeton Univ. Press, 1963).

4. For a more detailed discussion of this "bataille des fillières", see Saumon and Puiseux, "Actors and Decisions," pp. 146-49; and Irvin C. Bupp and Jean-Claude Derian, *Light Water* (New York: Basic Books, 1978), pp. 60-69.

5. See *France*, French Embassy Publication, March 1980 and Dec. 1980; *Atomwirtschaft*, Feb. 1979, p. 72.

6. See, for example, the series "Les Français devant le Choix Nucléaire" in *Le Monde* during Jan. 1975; the series "L'Energie du désespoir?" also in *Le Monde*, April 1975; and the series "Nucléaire: Le Grand Débat" in *Le Figaro*, May 1975.

7. Bupp and Derian, *Light Water*, p. 111.

8. Nelkin and Pollak, *Atom Besieged*, pp. 108-9.

9. For a more detailed comparison of the French and German antinuclear movements, see Nelkin and Pollak, *Atom Besieged*, especially chs. 8, 9, 10.

10. Bupp and Derian, *Light Water*, pp. 110-12.

11. Ibid., pp. 113-14.

12. Guy de Carmoy, "The new French energy policy," *Energy Policy* 10 (Sept. 1982): 185.

13. Andrew Shonfield, *Modern Capitalism*, p. 130.

14. Ibid., p. 128.

15. Stephen S. Cohen, *Modern Capitalist Planning*, p. 228.

16. Stanley Hoffmann, "The Paradoxes of the French Political Community," p. 91.

17. Saumon and Puiseux, "Actors and Decisions," p. 168.

18. For a detailed analysis of the operation of the PEON commission, see Philippe Simonnot, *Les Nucléocrates*, (Grenoble: Presses Universitaires de Grenoble, 1978).

19. Ibid., pp. 41-42, 47, 52.

20. Bupp and Derian, *Light Water*, p. 113.

21. Ibid., p. 112.

22. See *L'Electronucléaire en France*, a study sponsored by the CFDT and published by Editions du Seuil in 1975.

23. Bupp and Derian, *Light Water*, p. 117.

24. See, for example, Ezra N. Suleiman, *Elites in French Society* (Princeton, N.J.: Princeton Univ. Press, 1978); and Ezra N. Suleiman, *Politics, Power, and Bureaucracy in France* (Princeton, N.J.: Princeton Univ. Press, 1974).

25. Suleiman, *Elites in French Society*, p. 29.

26. Michel Debré commenting on the task of ENA; ibid., p. 41.

27. Cohen, *Modern Capitalist Planning*, pp. 50-51.

28. Suleiman, *Elites in French Society*, p. 161.

29. Decreasing France's energy dependence was a major theme of virtually every one of my more than twenty interviews conducted with French officials during early 1978 in all areas of the energy establishment. Similar responses were recorded by Simonnot in interviews with high officials from PEON. Simonnot, *Les Nucléocrates*, pp. 175-79.

30. See *The Economist*, 27 Dec. 1980, pp. 41-42.

31. These attitudes were reflected by the French officials whom I interviewed, and such convictions were also recorded by Simonnot from his interviews with PEON members; see *Les Nucléocrates*, pp. 179-80.

32. *Wall Street Journal*, 19 June 1979.

33. *Atomwirtschaft*, June 1980, p. 282.

34. For an analysis of French non-proliferation policy, see Pierre Lellouche, "France in the International Nuclear Energy Controversy: A New Policy under Giscard d'Estaing," *Orbis* 22 (Winter 1979): 951-65.

35. Ibid., p. 958. During this period there was an element of change in nuclear policy: the French quietly accepted the cancellation of their reprocessing contract by South Korea at the insistence of the United States.

36. *France's Position on Nuclear Proliferation*, French Embassy Press and Information Division, 80/8.

37. Lellouche, "France in the International Nuclear Energy Controversy," p. 959.

38. Ibid., p. 961.

39. See *San Francisco Examiner*, 9 Dec. 1984.

40. *The Economist*, 30 July 1983, p. 63; *San Francisco Examiner*, 9 Dec. 1984.

7. CONSENSUS POLITICS IN THE NETHERLANDS

1. According to at least one observer, however, this has perhaps been diminishing in recent years. See Arend Lijphart, *The Politics of Accommodation* (Berkeley and Los Angeles: Univ. of California Press, 1975).

2. The findings of the studies were summarized in the brochures "3500 MWe Kerncentrales in Nederland" and "Plaatsen voor Kerncentrales" published by Ministrie Van Economische Zaken, 1977.

3. See *Second Reflection Paper on Nuclear Energy*, Morgenster 5, Leusden, Holland, November 1975.

4. Smith and Spanhoff, "Nuclear Industry Debate in the Netherlands," p. 42.

5. Joerg Hallerbach, ed., *Die eigentliche Kernspaltung* (Darmstadt: Hermann Luchterhand Verlag, 1978), p. 227.

6. *News Bulletin*, the Hague, 10 Oct. 1974.

7. *Holland Herald* 5 (no. 4), 1980.

8. Smith and Spanhoff, "Nuclear Industry Debate in the Netherlands," p. 44.

9. *News Bulletin*, the Hague, 11 April 1978.

10. From an interview with Volker Hauff, Federal Minister for Research and Technology; *Der Spiegel*, 17 April 1978.

11. See *Summary of the Memorandum on Energy Policy: Part 2, the Coal Memorandum* (Ministry of Economic Affairs, February 1980).

12. See *Petroleum Economist*, March 1980. See *The Economist*, 11 Feb. 1984, p. 68; *Atomwirtschaft*, May 1984.

13. See *The Economist*, 11 Feb. 1984, p. 68; *Atomwirtschaft*, May 1984.

8. NUCLEAR POLITICS AND POLICYMAKING

1. For a discussion of these issues as they relate to the nuclear debate, see Nelkin and Pollak, *The Atom Besieged*.

2. This paradigm is perhaps most clearly articulated in the writings of Charles Lindblom. See Charles E. Lindblom, "The Science of 'Muddling Through'," *Public Administration Review* 19 (1959): 79-88; Charles E. Lindblom and David Braybrooke, *A Strategy of Decision* (New York: The Free Press, 1963).

3. See Todd R. LaPorte, "Managing Nuclear Waste," *Transaction, Social Science, and Modern Society* 18 (July/Aug., 1981): 57-65; Amatai Etzioni, "Mixed-Scanning: A 'Third' Approach to Decision-Making," *Public Administration Review* 27 (Dec. 1967); and Charles E. Lindblom, *Politics and Markets: The World's Political-Economic Systems* (New York: Basic Books, 1977).

Index

Achnacarry Agreement, 10
AEG (*Allgemeine Elektrizitaets Gesellschaft*), 82, 83
Ahaus, West Germany, 113, 135
Albrecht, Minister President, 112, 113, 114, 115, 116
Algeria, 18, 27, 30, 32, 61, 99, 207n
Almelo, Netherlands, 166, 179-81
alternative energy: nuclear power as, 2, 183; and oil dependence, 6; Dutch programs, 22, 60, 64, 185; and OPEC pricing, 33; French programs, 58
anti-nuclear movement: in West Germany, 71-76, 79, 103-09, 137-39, 211n; in France, 146-49, 158; in Netherlands, 172-76. *See also* environmentalism; nuclear power plants
Arab-Israeli War, 28
Aral, 28
Argentina, 134
Atomforum, 93
Atom Law, 137

BBU (*Bundersverband Buerger-initiativen Umweltschutz*), 74, 148
Belleville-sur-Loire, France, 158-9
Berlin Congress, 138
BMFT (*Bundesministerium fuer Forschung und Technologie*), 69, 131
Brazil-German deal, 83, 125-28, 179-82

British Petroleum, 9, 48, 50, 208n
Brokdorf, West Germany: demonstrations at, 74, 76, 87; court case, 80, 81; construction stop lifted, 135
Brown-Boveri, 178
Buergerdialog Kernenergie, 76-79
Bugey, France, 147
Bureau de Recherches de Pétrole, 15

Canada, 25, 28, 146
caramel, 166
Carter administration, 123-33, 165, 167-68
CDA (*Christen-Demokratisch Appel*), 65, 180, 181, 182, 184
CDU (*Christlich-Demokratische Union*), 105, 111, 112, 115, 139; CDU/CSU coalition, 106, 138, 213n
CEA (*Commissariat a l'Energie Atomique*), 143, 144
CFDT (*Confédération Française Démocratique du Travail*), 155
CFP (*Compagnie Francaise de Pétrole*), 9, 19, 28, 31, 57, 206n
CGT (*Confédération Générale du Travail*), 155
Charbonnages de France, 15
CNV (*Christelijk Nationaal Vakverbond in Nederland*), 174
coal, 2; and German energy policy, 11-14, 43, 44-46, 48, 150, 200; and French energy policy, 14, 15, 16, 17, 54, 58; and